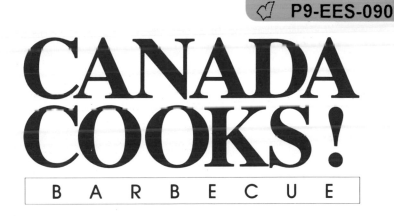

CANADA COOKS!

B A R B E C U E

by

Edena Sheldon

Whitecap Books

Published by
Whitecap Books Ltd.
1086 West 3rd Street
North Vancouver, B.C., Canada
V7P 3J6

Produced by Murray/Love Productions Inc.
1128 Homer Street
Vancouver, B.C., Canada
V6B 2X6

Canadian Cataloguing in Publication Data

Sheldon, Edena.
  Canada cooks : barbecue

  Includes index.
  ISBN 0-921061-19-6

  1. Barbecue cookery. I. Title
  TX840.B3S54 1988   641.5'784   C88-091253-7

Editor: Elaine Jones
Designer: David Counsell
Food Stylist: Edena Sheldon

Produced exclusively on the IBM Personal Publishing System
and IBM PS/2 Personal Systems.

All the props and accessories used in the photographs for this book were from the author's
own collection, Derik Murray and Marthe Love's collection, and from Barbecue Parts
Unlimited, Country Furniture, In Perspective, Kelly's Collection, Market Kitchen, Mikasa,
Ming Wo, Old Friends Antiques, and Scandinavian Antiques. Special thanks to Berni
Hastings, Brian Daisley, Judy Bates, Scott Wanless, Wendy Darling, Margaret Gibbs, John
Bishop, Howard Mah, and Darlene Hildebrandt for their hard work and invaluable
contributions.

Front Cover Photo: Florentine Grilled T-Bone Steak.

Printed in Canada by Friesen Printers.

CONTENTS

INTRODUCTION

Quite simply stated—*everything* seems to taste better hot off the grill. A steak has more "sizzle" done over fiery mesquite, juicy and rare with slightly charred edges, bursting with flavor. A burger is best done over hot coals, a crusty exterior sealing in a juicy rosy-red interior, ready to tuck into a toasty bun. Ribs have more "pizazz" infused with the smoky flavor of real hickory. And a thick slab of B.C. salmon hot off the grill and slathered with an herb-flecked butter is sublime. Well...you get the idea. The unabashed enthusiasm of this author for cooking *anything* on the barbecue is quite evident.

Hailing from my native Southern California, I have enjoyed my share of backyard get-togethers where the barbecue has taken center stage. Time was (in years past) when the art of barbecuing meant hot charcoal, smelly lighter fluid and a bottle of some red, smoky-flavored sauce. Now, I am the first to admit to very fond memories of burgers slathered with that sauce, of overdone hot-dogs, and too-rare chicken. But my childhood is also filled with memories of long skewers of Armenian lamb shish kebab prepared every Sunday by my father, of great picnics with several hundred guests (and a dozen barbecues going), of grilled fresh albacore stuffed with pine nuts and rice.

But today the art of barbecue has come a long way, to take its place as one of the staples of modern cooking. Nothing is simpler than coming home from a hectic day, lighting some coals and quickly grilling a steak or thick piece of fresh fish and some vegetables. I hope this book will bring barbecue into your life, to become more than a "weekend-only" event.

Finally, my thanks to Derik Murray, whose talent inspires my deepest respect and admiration. His keen eye, innovative eye for design and glorious photographs bring these recipes to life. Working together on this book (and enthusiastically devouring our "subjects" as we photographed them!) was a joy, and without Derik, this book would not have been possible.

In addition, I wish to thank my wonderful editor, Elaine Jones; Judy Bates, for her tasteful assistance in prop styling; Berni Hastings, for her good-humored patience and meticulous pagemaking; my designer/production manager, David Counsell, and Brian Daisley and Scott Wanless, who worked so enthusiastically with Derik and myself on the photos for the book. And special thanks to my husband, Gary, for his continued support and patience throughout all of my culinary projects.

So, let us begin. Armed with skewers and basting brushes let's get on to this popular way of cooking grilling on the barbecue!

BARBECUE BASICS

Memories are filled with occasions focusing on food. So many stories start out "remember when we had that terrific...," and tales of recent travels and trips always pass on that special little place with the great pasta, a fabulous sauce or a special dessert. My own honeymoon eighteen years ago was to a *restaurant* (Restaurant de la Pyramide, in Vienne, France, of the legendary Fernand Point)! But the happiest, most carefree, relaxed memories center on the barbecue—and the savory, simple and splendid food it puts forth.

As a squealing little girl, weenie roasts on the beach along the Pacific Ocean were the best! Charred edges, overcooked, too hot to bite into— one could eat one, two, three.... Even marshmallows done on a twig or long skewer were a form of barbecue, and in between those burnt fingertips and singed lips, they were the ultimate in taste thrills. Burgers off the grill, around someone's poolside, slathered with mustard and piled high with tomatoes and onions—they always seemed to require seconds and thirds (if no one was counting). There was nothing better.

The barbecue is part of my gastronomic heritage. My childhood was filled with Armenian barbecues, in our backyard, or in the yard of family or friends. Dad was always at the helm, preparing the coals to that perfect white-ash stage, skewering the lush chunks of lamb and colorful vegetables and doing it all to a perfect turn. Finally, my father would take a great chunk of Armenian *peda* bread and use it to push the cooked kebabs onto a large platter. My prize, for all my patience, was to share that juice-drenched piece of bread with my Dad. I can still, to this day, taste it.

My very first major magazine article was one I did years ago for *Sunset Magazine*—on how to give a blow-out barbecue for dozens of guests. I invited every cousin, aunt, uncle and good cook I knew—and they all came to Griffith Park in Los Angeles one Saturday. Everyone pitched in, *Sunset*'s art director and chief photographer flew in for the event, and it was the best barbecue I ever had. They documented, in eight full color pages, what we had been doing for years.

My barbecue went with me to Europe. Aromas wafted off our balcony in Frankfurt, driving our new German neighbors wild with curiosity. We shared our grill with new friends in Zürich; and we barbecued in Brussels. And in Nice, France, we enjoyed the special Niçoise way of grilling. To this day, my favorite grilled dish is dorade, a native mediterranean fish, grilled over dried fennel branches, in the manner of Nice. I had it several times weekly and never tired of it.

So, to get you started on your own store of happy memories of grilling, here are some Barbecue Basics—an updated approach to our oldest form of cooking!

ON SELECTING YOUR BARBECUE

The best barbecued steak I ever had was cooked on the most primitive grill imaginable. It was in a tiny restaurant in Brussels, on a very rainy, blustery February evening. A hundred-year-old stone fireplace was tucked into the corner of the straw-strewn stone floor. An ancient, not-so-stable grill was set right over the oak logs, balancing on three legs. Our thick prime beefsteaks were done on that fire, and served to us on oversized pottery plates with a plum-sized ball of fresh Belgian butter on top, which quickly melted over the slightly charred surface—proof positive that the most humble of equipment can produce memorable results.

For today's barbecue enthusiast, there is a myriad of wonderful grills to choose from, in every style and price range. The types are four basic barbecue styles:

The Open Brazier: An uncovered grill, sometimes equipped with a hood. Table-top Japanese hibachis are considered a type of brazier. It is basically a pan to hold the fire, with a grill on top of it. When selecting a brazier, an adjustable grill is useful, to help regulate heat. Braziers are meant for open-air grilling over direct heat. This type is the "grand-daddy" of grills.

The Covered Barbecue Grill: This type of barbecue is the popular, rounded two-piece grill, known as the "kettle." It comes on legs or wheels and is available in a range of sizes (18" (45 cm) and 24" (60 cm) being the most popular). On this type, dampers on the lid and firebox allow simple regulation of necessary air flow and amount of heat. Covered, the kettle can easily do whole birds, large roasts and whole fish—working much like an oven does. Uncovered, this type of grill works on the same principle as the open brazier.

The Grill Wagon: This is the popular, deluxe barbecue type, for the serious chef. Covered, on giant wheels, it can be moved around with ease. Often complete with carving boards, rotisserie spits, elevated warming shelves and swing-up work surfaces. Complete with dampers and vents to regulate heat precisely. The heavy, fitted lid makes the very most out of aromatic woods and herbs.

Gas Barbecues: This type of grill offers total convenience. This is the beauty that makes barbecue a breeze, giving the cook fire when needed, with no waiting, no fuss, no muss and not much clean-up. Gas barbe-

1

cues come equipped with their natural or bottled (propane) gas. (Out-door units that can be moved around and are outfitted with bottled gas are my preference. Natural gas units must be permanently connected to a gas line.) Special lava or ceramic "briquets" are heated by the gas flame, and cook exactly like charcoal. Meat juices drip on these briquets and the smoke rises, resulting in the barbecue flavor. Many swear they cannot tell the difference between real charcoal-grilled food and that done over gas—the real purists will never admit to it, however!

THE HEAT IS ON
Hot describes coals partially covered with grey ashes. You will be able to hold your hand over these coals for 3 seconds.

Medium-hot describes coals that glow red through a layer of grey ashes. You will be able to hold your hand over these coals for 5 seconds.

Low describes coals completely covered with a layer of ashes, with no glow at all peeking through. You will be able to hold your hand over these coals for 6–7 seconds.

To raise temperature, push coals closer together and knock some of the ashes off. Fan with a folded-up newspaper until they glow. To lower temperature, separate the coals into a single layer with spaces between the coals. Raise the grill higher, or try misting with water.

TOOLS OF THE TRADE
Your supply of necessary barbecue tools may be very simple or very elaborate with gadgets galore. The essentials to a good barbecue are:

Tongs: Long-handled, for turning meats and poultry. Never pierce meats by turning with a fork, as juices will escape.

Metal Pancake Turner: Flat, no holes, for turning pieces of fish, vegetables, fruits.

Pot Holder and Mitts: Heavy-duty, preferably of non-flammable material.

Meat Thermometer: The new, slender, needle-like, "instant-reading" types are terrific for testing internal heat of meats. Insert in thickest part.

Basting Brushes: Possibly the single most important tool for the barbecue chef. Get long-handled ones, both fine-bristled and wide, paint-brush types for larger birds. Wash well and dry completely between uses, and they should last a long time.

Water Spritzer: For dousing out flames in an instant; for fat-dripping flare-ups, or sudden bursts of flames.

Bib Apron with Pockets: Tuck a nice kitchen towel in at the waist, convenient for hand-wiping—something you'll be doing a lot of.

Hinged Wire Basket: The type that opens up like a book is great for holding a good supply of burgers, smaller fish, shrimp, small chops and chicken wings.

Skewers: A selection of long metal skewers for meats and kebabs; shorter metal skewers and bamboo skewers for appetizers and individual portions. Soak wooden skewers in water for 15–20 minutes before using, to prevent burning on the grill.

Wire Brush: This is essential. The grill must be scraped clean every time before grilling. Use the steel plate on top of the brush to scrape off tough char, and the brush itself to clean the rack. Run under very hot water to clean, and shake completely dry to prevent rusting.

WHICH FUEL...AND THE NEW AROMATIC WOODS

Charcoal is still king! Select charcoal or charcoal briquets, or any of the special hardwood charcoals (oak, maple, cherry, hickory, mesquite). Oak and hickory charcoal produce aromatic, flavorful smoke. *Aromatic woods* may also be used for grilling, although they do not burn as hot as charcoal. Select from *cherry; alderwood* (popular in the Pacific Northwest and in B.C. for salmon with a subtle, light, smoky flavor); *mesquite* (the rage of the 80s from the Southwest, known for its hot-burning, sizzling heat and very intense, smoky flavor—great for hearty ribs, steaks and ckicken); *hickory* (produces a very smoky, intense aroma); *oak* (medium smoky flavor, for burgers, chicken, fish, lamb); and *applewood* (gives a nutty, sweet flavor to chicken, fish, shellfish, ham, bacon, sausages—applewood-smoked turkey is a New England specialty). Flavored chips of these aromatic woods can give just the right amount of flavor and are an efficient way of flavoring meats; soak first in warm water before tossing on hot coals.

RARE, MEDIUM OR WELL DONE?

I have my own sure-fire method for testing when meat is done precisely rare, medium or well-done. Use this simple finger test: press the cooking meat, fish or poultry with your index finger.

Rare: The meat will feel soft (almost squishy), and your finger will leave hardly a trace of indentation.

Medium Rare: The meat will feel a bit firmer, with some resistance, and feel slightly "springy."

Well-Done: If you must have your meat well-done, it will feel very firm when pressed.

ON GRILLING VEGETABLES AND FRUITS

Almost any vegetable or fruit may be grilled right alongside your meat, fish or poultry. They are instant side-dishes, provide color and flavor, and are almost at their best when grilled. I have provided suggested bastes and sauces throughout the book—but my all-time favorite is to brush vegetables with olive oil (or a combination of olive oil and melted butter), and grill simply, perhaps with a sprinkle of herbs, or with salt and pepper.

Cook and turn vegetables frequently until they are streaked with golden-brown grill marks and test just tender when pressed. Serve hot, warm or at room temperature. Suggested vegetables for grilling are:

Bell peppers: Rinse, dry, cut in half and grill, brushing with olive oil.

Carrots: Grill whole or halved, brushing with butter.

Fresh Corn: (see Great Grilling Partners, page 141).

Eggplants: Japanese variety, grill whole. Globe variety, grill in quarters. On both, leave skin and stem-end intact. Brush with oil.

Leeks and Scallions: Grill whole, brushing with oil-butter.

Mushrooms: Wipe clean with damp cloth; do not soak in water. Thread on skewers, and grill whole, brushing with oil-butter.

Onions: Halve or cut in thick slices. Brush with olive oil and grill, turning with a metal spatula. May be grilled in a hinged basket.

Potatoes: All varieties, including sweet potatoes and yams. Cut in halves, thick slices, or wedges. Grill, brushing with butter-oil.

Radicchio: (see Great Grilling Partners, page 141).

Squash: All varieties (zucchini, crookneck, patty pan). Grill whole, or split open lengthwise. Brush with olive oil and herbs.

Tomatoes: Grill in halves, turning with a metal spatula. Thread cherry tomatoes on a skewer and grill. Brush with butter-oil.

Fruits are delightful grilled, and add a colorful, flavorful accent to barbecued meats, fish and poultry. Use the suggested sauces or bastes or brush with simple melted butter or a flavored butter. Fruits should be grilled until just tender, with lovely golden grill markings. Serve warm or cool.

Suggested fruits for grilling are:

Apples: Core, halve or quarter. Or bake whole, wrapped in foil (see Great Grilling Partners, page 141), brushing with butter.

Apricots: Cut in half, discard seed, grill flat. Brush with butter.

Bananas: Cut in half lengthwise (do not peel). Brush cut side with butter.

Melons: All varieties (canteloupe, Persian, honeydew), cut into thick wedges. Brush with citrus-butter.

Nectarines: Cut in half, grill flat, discarding pit. Brush with butter.

Papayas: Peel and quarter. Grill, brushing with butter.

Pears: Halve or quarter, grill, brushing with butter.

Pineapple: Peel and core. Slice pineapple into thick rings or long wedges. Grill, brushing with butter.

MARINADES, FLAVORED BUTTERS, SAUCES AND GLAZES

When it comes to barbecue—the sauce is the thing! The carefully chosen steak—slab or ribs—or thick fresh fish steak is the (all-important) supporting cast, but the sauce or marinade takes center stage with the starring role. Our supermarket shelves groan under the weight of excellent prepared hickory sauces, teriyaki marinades, chutney glazes and prepared salsas. But preparing your own is not only satisfying and fun—the results are well worth it from first bite. A pantry full of good olive oil, a selection of flavorful herbs and spices, some leftover wine and an array of marmalades and preserves are all you need to get started. When fresh herbs are on hand, they need only be combined with butter for marvelous, savory butters to serve chilled as toppings for sizzling grilled meats. Barbecue sauces may be prepared days and weeks in advance, kept refrigerated and used at a minute's notice. They're all here—some 43 recipes to get you started, the largest chapter in the book, the "meat" of my message. Don't be timid—dig right in and try these, then create your own. This is the fun part of the whole barbecue scene.

HERBED OLIVE OIL
AND LEMON MARINADE

*This fresh, zesty marinade is especially appealing with thick veal chops, veal breast, loin pork and chicken. Use a fruity olive oil, fresh lemon juice and fresh sage leaves. **Makes 1 1/2 cups (375 mL).***

1/2 cup (125 mL)	fruity olive oil
1/3 cup (75 mL)	fresh lemon juice
	grated rind from 1 large lemon
	(yellow part only)
1/3 cup (75 mL)	dry Vermouth
2 cloves	fresh garlic, peeled and pressed
2 tbsp. (30 mL)	minced fresh sage leaves
1 tsp. (5 mL)	cracked black peppercorns

Whisk all ingredients together in a food processor, or by hand, until smooth and emulsified. Use as needed.

MARSALA
AND OLIVE OIL MARINADE

*This sophisticated, upscale marinade derives its smoky, earthy flavor from Marsala—a fortified red wine from Italy, much like Sherry in flavor. These flavorings team beautifully with grilled chicken breasts, game hens or quail, veal chops and T-bones. **Makes 2 cups (500 mL).***

1 1/3 cups (325 mL)	Marsala
1/3 cup (75 mL)	very fruity olive oil
4 tbsp. (60 mL)	fresh lemon juice
2 tbsp. (30 mL)	fresh oregano leaves
1 large clove	garlic, peeled and pressed
1 tsp. (5 mL)	cracked black peppercorns
1 tbsp. (15 mL)	minced fresh parsley

Whisk all ingredients together in a food processor, or by hand, until smooth and emulsified. Use as needed.

"MARTINI" MARINADE

*This is an amusing name for a very good marinade. Using two stand-bys for a classic martini—Gin and Vermouth—this marinade is great with game (especially a loin of venison), game birds and poutry, dark-meat turkey and pork. **Makes 1 1/2 cups (375 mL).***

3/4 cup (175 mL)	Gin
1/4 cup (50 mL)	dry Vermouth
1/3 cup (75 mL)	olive oil
16	juniper berries
2	bay leaves, crumbled
1/2 tsp. (2 mL)	cracked black peppercorns
2 tbsp. (30 mL)	fresh lemon juice
2 tsp. (10 mL)	finely grated lemon zest (yellow part only)

Whisk all ingredients together in a food processor, or by hand, until smooth and emulsified. Use as needed.

WHITE WINE HERBED MARINADE

*This marinade is excellent for all kinds of chicken and poultry, for shellfish, salmon, trout, swordfish and other sturdy fish. Select the fresh herb that suits you. **Makes 1 1/2 cups (375 mL).***

2/3 cup (150 mL)	dry white wine
1/3 cup (75 mL)	best-quality, white wine vinegar
1/2 cup (125 mL)	olive oil
3 tbsp. (45 mL)	minced, fresh tarragon, rosemary, basil, thyme or dill
1 small clove	garlic, peeled and pressed
2 tbsp. (30 mL)	finely minced shallots

Whisk all ingredients together in a food processor, or by hand, until smooth and emulsified. Use as needed.

PEPPERED RED WINE MARINADE

This marinade is excellent for lamb, flank steak, all cuts of beef and pork. Select any fresh herb that suits you and the kind of meat you will be grilling. **Makes 1 1/2 cups (375 mL).**

2/3 cup (75 mL)	dry red wine (Cabernet, Zinfandel, Pinot Noir, Burgundy)
1/4 cup (50 mL)	best-quality red wine vinegar
2 tbsp. (30 mL)	balsamic vinegar
1/2 cup (125 mL)	olive oil
1/4 cup (50 mL)	minced red onion
1 large clove	garlic, peeled and pressed
2	bay leaves, crumbled
2 tsp. (5 mL)	cracked black peppercorns
2 tbsp. (30 mL)	minced fresh rosemary, tarragon, thyme or oregano

Whisk all ingredients together in a food processor, or by hand, until smooth and emulsified. Use as needed.

MEXICAN FRESH LIME MARINADE

This marinade comes from south of the border and adds a wonderful, authentic flavor to swordfish, shellfish and chicken. The flavor is tangy, refreshing and addictive. **Makes 1 1/2 cups (375 mL).**

1/2 cup (125 mL)	fresh lime juice
1/3 cup (75 mL)	olive oil
1/3 cup (75 mL)	beer
1 tbsp. (15 mL)	finely grated lime zest
1 tbsp. (15 mL)	white wine vinegar
1 tbsp. (15 mL)	honey
1/4 cup (50 mL)	minced scallions (white part only)
1/3 cup (75 mL)	minced fresh cilantro leaves (Chinese parsley, fresh coriander)

Whisk all ingredients together in a food processor, or by hand, until smooth and emulsified. Use as needed.

PORT AND APPLE MARINADE

This fresh-tasting marinade is terrific for turkey, game, pork and duck. The flavors of apple cider, Port, spices and flavorings provide an exciting contrast to these rich meats. The slightly charred flavor from the hot grill adds another dimension and the result is a sure-fire winner.
Makes 3 cups (750 mL).

1/2 cup (125 mL)	minced red onion
1 cup (250 mL)	apple cider
1/4 cup (50 mL)	applejack (Apple Brandy or Calvados)
1/2 cup (125 mL)	Port
1/2 cup (125 mL)	apple cider vinegar
1/3 cup (75 mL)	honey
1/2 cup (125 mL)	safflower oil
2 cloves	garlic, peeled and crushed
1 tsp. (5 mL)	ground allspice
2 tbsp. (30 mL)	juniper berries
2 tsp. (10 mL)	cracked black peppercorns
6 sprigs	*each* fresh rosemary, sage and thyme

Heat together the red onion, cider, applejack, Port, vinegar and honey in a small, deep stainless steel saucepan. Bring to a simmer and cook 15 minutes. Remove from heat and cool to room temperature. Stir in the oil, garlic, allspice, juniper berries, pepper and fresh herbs. Use as needed.

JAPANESE TERIYAKI MARINADE

This popular marinade is great on steaks, burgers, flank steak, chicken and pork chops. **Makes 1 1/2 cups (375 mL).**

1/2 cup (125 mL)	soy sauce
1/3 cup (75 mL)	peanut oil
1/3 cup (75 mL)	Sherry
4 tbsp. (60 mL)	honey
2 cloves	garlic, peeled and pressed
2 tbsp. (30 mL)	finely grated fresh ginger
1 tbsp. (15 mL)	Sherry wine vinegar
1/3 cup (75 mL)	scallions, trimmed and very thinly sliced

Whisk all ingredients together in a food processor, or by hand, until smooth and emulsified. Use as needed.

PROVENÇAL MARINADE

This marinade evokes the French Riviera—full of all those familiar flavors of olive oil, garlic, fragrant herbs native to the area and fresh lemon. This is a creamy, substantial marinade for basting chicken, veal riblets, lamb racks, and swordfish steaks. **Makes 1 1/2 cups (375 mL).**

1/3 cup (75 mL)	fresh lemon juice
1/4 cup (50 mL)	red wine vinegar
2 tbsp. (30 mL)	finely grated lemon rind
4 large cloves	garlic, peeled and pressed
2 tbsp. (30 mL)	dried herbes de provençe
1/3 cup (75 mL)	Dijon mustard
1/2 cup (125 mL)	olive oil

Whisk together the lemon juice, vinegar, lemon rind, garlic and dried herbs until smooth and well blended. Whisk in the mustard until very smooth. In a slow, steady stream, whisk in the olive oil. Set aside until ready to use as desired.

CITRUS AND SAGE MARINADE

This is a wonderful, fresh-tasting marinade for duck, turkey, chicken, pork and veal. Marinate for a full 24 hours to allow flavors to permeate meat before grilling. **Makes 1 1/2 cups (375 mL).**

1 whole	lemon, ground (including rind)
1 small	orange, ground (including rind)
1/2 cup (125 mL)	olive oil
2 tbsp. (30 mL)	honey
12	fresh sage leaves, minced
2 cloves	garlic, peeled and minced
2 tbsp. (30 mL)	red wine vinegar
1 tsp. (5 mL)	cracked black peppercorns

Whisk all ingredients together in a food processor until grainy-smooth and emulsified. Use as needed.

Opposite: (From center front) Pork Rub Dry Seasoning Mix, Garlic and Herbed Lemon Butter, Apricot Barbecue Sauce, Real Texas Barbecue Sauce, White Wine Herbed Marinade, Peppered Red Wine Herbed Marinade, Orange Curry Mustard Marinade, Fresh Basil Pesto.

FAR EAST ORIENTAL
SESAME MARINADE

This sultry, smoky marinade is great with flank steak, poultry, duck and pork tenderloin. Its wonderful flavor holds up particularly well to grilling. **Makes a generous 2 cups (500 mL).**

1 cup (250 mL)	dry red wine
1/3 cup (75 mL)	sesame oil (available where Oriental foods are sold)
1/3 cup (75 mL)	peanut oil
1/4 cup (50 mL)	red wine vinegar
6	scallions (spring onions), trimmed and finely minced
2 large cloves	garlic, peeled and pressed
2 tbsp. (30 mL)	finely grated fresh ginger
2 tbsp. (30 mL)	brown sugar, packed
1 tbsp. (15 mL)	fresh thyme leaves

Whisk all ingredients together in a food processor, or by hand, until smooth and emulsified. Use as needed.

ORANGE-SOY MARINADE
WITH HONEY

This marinade is terrific on butterflied Cornish game hens, chicken, duck and pork ribs. The slightly sweet citrus flavor is very appealing, and the final result is sticky, pleasantly charred and smoky tasting.
Makes a generous 2 cups (500 mL).

2/3 cup (150 mL)	*fresh* orange juice
	grated rind from 1 orange
1/3 cup (75 mL)	Sherry
1/4 cup (50 mL)	Sherry wine vinegar
1/3 cup (75 mL)	peanut oil
3 tbsp. (45 mL)	honey
3 tbsp. (45 mL)	finely grated fresh ginger
4 tbsp. (60 mL)	light soy sauce.

Whisk all ingredients together in a food processor, or by hand, until smooth and emulsified. Use as needed.

ORANGE-CURRY MUSTARD MARINADE

This is a refreshing, slightly spicy, slightly sweet marinade for chicken, turkey and all cuts of pork and pork ribs. **Makes 1 2/3 cups (400 mL) marinade.**

1 cup (250 mL)	fresh squeezed oranged juice
2 tbsp. (30 mL)	grated orange rind (orange part only)
2 tbsp. (30 mL)	Dijon-style mustard
2 tbsp. (30 mL)	grainy mustard
1 tbsp. (15 mL)	curry powder
1 tsp. (5 mL)	salt
1 tsp. (5 mL)	cracked black peppercorns
2 tbsp. (30 mL)	cider vinegar
2 tbsp. (30 mL)	vegetable oil

Whisk together all the ingredients in a small jar until completely blended and smooth. Use as desired.

KRÄUTER BUTTER (FRESH HERBED BUTTER)

When I lived in Germany and Switzerland, my local supermarkets always carried a wonderful butter "log," flecked with fresh herbs, called Kräuter Butter (herbed butter)—ready to slice and top grilled or broiled chops, fish, steaks or chicken. It made a simple meat very special. Keep this butter on hand, chilled for the same uses. **Makes 1 1/2 cups (375 mL).**

3/4 pound (375 grams)	very fresh butter, softened
2 tbsp. (30 mL)	*each* minced fresh chives, thyme, dillweed and parsley
2 tbsp. (30 mL)	fresh lemon juice
2 small cloves	fresh garlic, peeled and pressed
1/2 tsp. (2 mL)	paprika

In a food processor, combine the butter, fresh herbs, lemon juice, garlic and paprika. Beat until fluffy and well incorporated. Store butter in a tightly sealed crock, or form into a "log" and wrap in waxed paper. Chill several hours, overnight, or for up to one week before using. May be frozen for one month.

LEMON BUTTER

Keep this zesty, lemon-flavored butter on hand in the refrigerator. Slice off a big chunk and place it on a hot, succulent piece of fish right off the grill. It is delicious. **Makes 1 cup (250 mL).**

1/2 pound (250 grams)	very fresh butter, just softened
4 tbsp. (60 mL)	fresh lemon juice
	grated rind from 1 large lemon (yellow part only)
2 tbsp. (30 mL)	finely minced fresh parsley

Cream the softened butter. Add the lemon juice, lemon rind and fresh parsley and continue to beat until fluffy and well incorporated. (A food processor is ideal for this recipe.) Store butter in a tightly sealed crock, or form into a "log" and wrap in waxed paper. Chill several hours, or overnight, or for up to one week before using. May be frozen for one month.

GARLIC AND HERBED LEMON BUTTER

Keep this savory butter on hand in the refrigerator to top a sizzling burger, piece of succulent fish, or a thick veal chop right off the grill. **Makes 1 cup (250 mL).**

1/2 pound (250 grams)	very fresh butter, softened
2 large cloves	fresh garlic, peeled and pressed
3 tbsp. (45 mL)	snipped fresh mixed herbs (dill, sage, oregano, marjoram, thyme, parsley), finely minced
1 tbsp. (15 mL)	snipped fresh chives, finely minced
3 tbsp. (45 mL)	fresh lemon juice
	grated rind from 1 large lemon (yellow part only)

Cream the softened butter. Add the garlic, mixed herbs, chives, lemon juice and lemon rind. Continue to beat until fluffy and well incorporated. (A food processor is ideal for this recipe.) Store butter in a tightly sealed crock, or form into a "log" and wrap in waxed paper. Chill several hours, overnight or for up to one week before using. May be frozen for one month.

ROSEMARY-ORANGE-CURRANT BUTTER

Keep this savory butter chilled and on hand to top a sizzling swordfish steak, lamb chop, duck or chicken. It is also delicious served over hot grilled squash, corn or potatoes. **Makes 1 1/3 cups (325 mL).**

1/2 pound (250 grams)	very fresh butter, softened
1/3 cup (75 mL)	dried currants soaked in warm water 10 minutes and drained
1 small clove	fresh garlic, peeled and pressed
3 tbsp. (45 mL)	fresh orange juice
2 tbsp. (30 mL)	finely grated orange rind (orange part only)
3 tbsp. (45 mL)	fresh rosemary leaves
1 tbsp. (15 mL)	balsamic or Sherry wine vinegar freshly ground coarse black peppercorns

Cream the softened butter. Add the drained currants, garlic, orange juice, orange rind, rosemary leaves and vinegar. Continue to beat until fluffy and well incorporated. (A food processor is ideal for this recipe.) Store butter in a tightly sealed crock, or form into a "log" and wrap in waxed paper. Chill several hours, overnight, or for up to one week before using. May be frozen for one month.

GREEN PEPPERCORN-LIME BUTTER

This is a lively butter that is a treat on grilled fresh salmon, swordfish or thick, juicy pork chops. Simple to prepare, this butter turns a simple grill into something very special. **Makes 1 generous cup (250 mL).**

1/2 pound (250 grams)	very fresh butter, softened
3 tbsp. (45 mL)	green peppercorns, drained (imported from Madagascar or France, packed in brine and sold in small jars)
3 tbsp. (45 mL)	fresh lime juice
1 tbsp. (15 mL)	finely grated lime rind (green part only)
2 tbsp. (30 mL)	minced fresh parsley
	salt

Using a food processor, cream together the butter, drained green peppercorns, lime juice, lime rind and parsley. Beat until fluffy and well incorporated. Season to taste with salt, if needed. Store butter in a tighty sealed crock, or form into a "log" and wrap in waxed paper. Chill several hours, overnight, or for up to one week before using. May be frozen for one month.

GINGER-LIME BUTTER

This flavored butter is great to keep on hand, chilled, to top a piece of grilled fresh fish of any kind as it comes off the coals. It is especially delicious on lobster, swordfish, monkfish—and any cut of chicken. **Makes 1 cup (250 mL).**

1/2 pound (250 grams)	very fresh butter, softened
2 tbsp. (30 mL)	minced fresh ginger
2 tsp. (10 mL)	finely grated fresh lime rind
2 tbsp. (30 mL)	fresh lime juice
1 small clove	garlic, peeled and pressed
2 tbsp. (30 mL)	minced fresh parsley
	freshly ground white peppercorns

Cream the softened butter. Add the ginger, lime rind, lime juice, garlic and parsley. Continue to beat until fluffy and well incorporated. (A food processor is ideal for this recipe.) Season to taste with white pepper. Store butter in a tightly sealed crock, or form into a "log" and wrap in waxed paper. Chill several hours, overnight or for up to one week before using. May be frozen for one month.

DOUBLE-MUSTARD BUTTER

This savory butter is spiked with Dijon mustard and has the added crunch of whole mustard seeds. Serve slathered over grilled turkey breast, pork chops or chicken. **Makes 1 1/2 cups (375 mL).**

1/2 pound (250 grams)	very fresh butter, softened
1/3 cup (75 mL)	fresh parsley, finely minced
2 tbsp. (30 mL)	minced fresh chives
4 tbsp. (60 mL)	Dijon mustard
2 tbsp. (30 mL)	whole mustard seeds
2 tsp. (10 mL)	finely grated lemon rind (yellow part only)
	coarsely ground black peppercorns

Using a food processor, cream together the softened butter, parsley, chives, mustard, mustard seeds and lemon rind. Beat until fluffy and well incorporated. Season to taste with black pepper. Store butter in a tightly sealed crock, or form into a "log" and wrap in waxed paper. Chill several hours, overnight, or for up to one week before using. May be frozen for one month.

FRESH BASIL-MUSTARD BUTTER

This wonderful, fresh basil- and mustard-spiked butter is great to have on hand to top hot grilled vegetables, pasta, grilled seafood, veal chops or poultry. **Makes 1 1/2 cups (375 mL).**

1 small clove	garlic, peeled and pressed
1 cup (250 mL)	fresh basil leaves, packed
1/2 tsp. (2 mL)	salt
1/2 pound (250 grams)	very fresh butter, softened
2 tbsp. (30 mL)	Dijon mustard
1 tbsp. (15 mL)	fresh lemon juice

Using a food processor, purée the garlic, basil and salt to a coarse paste. Beat in the softened butter, mustard and lemon juice. Beat until fluffy and well incorporated. Store butter in a tightly sealed crock, or form into a "log" and wrap in waxed paper. Chill several hours, overnight, or for up to one week before using. May be frozen for one month.

SAVORY WATERCRESS-MUSTARD BUTTER

This spicy butter is as good as the watercress you find—the nippier, the better. Prepare up to three days in advance, and chill until ready to use. **Makes 1 cup (250 mL).**

1/2 pound (250 grams)	very fresh butter, softened
1 1/4 cups (300 grams)	watercress, coarsely chopped and packed
1 clove	garlic, peeled and pressed
2 tbsp. (30 mL)	fresh parsley leaves, minced
2 tbsp. (30 mL)	finely minced shallots
3 tbsp. (45 mL)	Dijon mustard
	few drops liquid hot-pepper sauce (Tabasco)
1 tbsp. (15 mL)	fresh lemon juice
	salt
	freshly ground black and white peppercorns

In a food processor, cream together the butter, watercress, garlic, parsley and shallots until well blended, scraping down sides frequently with a rubber scraper. Add the mustard, hot-pepper sauce and lemon juice, and continue to blend. Season to taste with salt and pepper. Store flavored butter in a tightly sealed crock or form into a "log" and wrap in waxed paper. Chill several hours, overnight or for up to three days before using. May be frozen for one month.

SPICY TOMATO BUTTER

*This spicy, tomato-flavored butter is a beautiful rosy color and is delicious melted over a thick piece of sturdy grilled fish, such as bluefish, swordfish, shark or mahi-mahi. **Makes 1 1/2 cups (375 mL).***

4	shallots
4 tbsp. (60 mL)	red wine vinegar
1 tbsp. (15 mL)	dried oregano leaves
1 tsp. (5 mL)	thyme leaves
2 tbsp. (30 mL)	water
1/2 pound (250 grams)	very fresh butter, softened
3 tbsp. (45 mL)	tomato paste
	pinch sugar

In a small, stainless steel saucepan, heat the shallots, vinegar, oregano, thyme and water over medium heat. Simmer until 2 tbsp. (30 mL) liquid remains and shallots are tender. Allow mixture to cool completely.

In a food processor, beat together the softened butter, tomato paste, pinch sugar and cooled shallot mixture. Beat until fluffy and well incorporated. Store butter in a tightly sealed crock, or form into a "log" and wrap in waxed paper. Chill several hours, overnight, or for up to one week before using. May be frozen for one month.

PUNGENT OLIVE BUTTER

*Keep this savory, pungent, olive-flavored butter on hand in the refrigerator to top grilled fish, lamb chops or grilled vegetables. The color is confetti-like, and the flavor is Spanish in inspiration. **Makes 1 1/2 cups (375 mL).***

1/2 pound (250 grams)	very fresh butter, softened
2 cloves	garlic, peeled and pressed
1/2 cup (125 mL)	sliced, pimiento-stuffed green olives
2 tbsp. (30 mL)	capers, drained
3 tbsp. (45 mL)	pimiento, drained
1/4 cup (50 mL)	minced fresh parsley
2 tbsp. (30 mL)	Sherry wine vinegar
	salt
	freshly ground black pepper

Using a food processor, beat together the softened butter, garlic, olives, capers, pimiento, parsley and vinegar. Beat until fluffy and well incorporated. Season to taste with salt and pepper. Store butter in a tightly sealed crock, or form into a "log" and wrap in waxed paper. Chill several hours, overnight or for up to one week before using. May be frozen for one month.

GREEN CHILI BUTTER

This hot-spiced flavored butter is great served chilled over a sizzling char-grilled veal chop or chicken breast. Simple to make, keep this butter on hand to turn a simple grill into something with pizazz.
Makes 1 1/2 cups (375 mL).

4 large	Anaheim peppers
1 very small	jalapeño pepper
1 tsp. (5 mL)	salt
1 large clove	garlic, peeled and pressed
1/2 pound (250 grams)	very fresh butter, softened
2 tbsp. (30 mL)	fresh lime juice
2 tbsp. (30 mL)	minced fresh parsley

Brush the Anaheim peppers and jalapeño lightly with corn oil, and broil 4–5 minutes until charred, turning on all sides. Place peppers in a brown paper bag and close tightly to "steam" skins loose, 15 minutes. When peppers are cool enough to handle, remove stems, skins and seeds. (Handle peppers carefully; wash hands, and do not rub eyes or face.)

In a food processor, purée the peppers, salt and garlic. Beat in the softened butter, lime juice and parsley until fluffy and well incorporated. Store butter in a tightly sealed crock, or form into a "log" and wrap in waxed paper. Chill several hours, overnight or for up to one week before using. May be frozen for one month.

GORGONZOLA BUTTER

This savory, assertive butter—spiked with creamy, sharp Gorgonzola cheese—is made for grilled beef steaks. Keep on hand in the refrigerator to slice and top a sizzling steak, hot off the grill. This butter is also delicious over fresh green beans, hot grilled corn and (especially!) on baked or grilled potatoes.
Makes 2 cups (500 mL).

1/2 pound (250 grams)	very fresh butter, softened
8 ounces (250 grams)	creamy, soft, imported, Gorgonzola cheese, crumbled and at room temperature
1 small clove	garlic, peeled and minced
1 tsp. (5 mL)	cracked black peppercorns
2 tbsp. (30 mL)	minced fresh parsley

Using a food processor, cream together all the ingredients. Beat until fluffy and well incorporated. Season to taste with salt, if needed. Store butter in a tightly sealed crock, or form into a "log" and wrap in waxed paper. Chill several hours, overnight or for up to one week before using. May be frozen for one month.

PARMESAN-GARLIC BUTTER

This butter is great to slather over hot grilled swordfish, halibut, fresh red snapper or split lobsters. It is equally delicious over corn, eggplant, zucchini and tomatoes. ***Makes 2 cups (500 mL).***

1/2 pound (250 grams)	very fresh butter, softened
2 cloves	garlic, peeled and minced
2/3 cup (150 mL)	freshly grated Parmesan cheese
1/2 cup (125 mL)	finely minced fresh parsley

Using a food processor, cream together all the ingredients. Beat until fluffy and well incorporated. Season to taste with salt, if needed. Store butter in a tightly sealed crock, or form into a "log" and wrap in waxed paper. Chill several hours, overnight or for up to one week before using. May be frozen for one month.

HORSERADISH BUTTER

*This nippy butter is great served in a chilled slice over a sizzling steak. It also transform a thick, juicy beef burger into something special. **Makes 1 1/4 cups (300 mL).***

1/2 pound (250 grams)	very fresh butter, softened
4 tbsp. (60 mL)	prepared horseradish (not the creamed variety)
1 tbsp. (15 mL)	Dijon mustard
	salt
	freshly ground black pepper
1 tbsp. (15 mL)	minced fresh parsley

Using a food processor, cream together the butter, prepared horseradish and mustard. Beat until fluffy and well incorporated. Season to taste with salt and pepper, and beat in the minced parsley. Store butter in a tightly sealed crock, or form into a "log" and wrap in waxed paper. Chill several hours, overnight or for up to one week before using. May be frozen for one month.

PERNOD BUTTER

*This delicious savory butter is reminiscent of the French Riviera—flavored with anise-flavored Pernod liqueur, fennel seeds, tarragon, shallots and lemon. Keep chilled in a "log" and slice off to top sizzling grilled fish steaks or grilled fresh oysters. **Makes 1 1/4 cups (300 mL).***

1/2 pound (250 grams)	very fresh butter, softened
4 tbsp. (60 mL)	Pernod liqueur (or Anisette)
2 tsp. (10 mL)	whole fennel seed, crushed
3 tbsp. (45 mL)	minced fresh tarragon leaves
	grated rind from 1 lemon
2 tbsp. (30 mL)	minced shallots
	salt
	freshly ground black pepper

Using a food processor, cream together the butter, Pernod, fennel seeds, tarragon leaves, lemon rind and shallots. Beat until fluffy and well incorporated. Season to taste with salt and pepper. Store butter in a tightly sealed crock, or form into a "log" and wrap in waxed paper. Chill several hours, overnight or for up to one week before using. May be frozen for one month.

REAL TEXAS BARBECUE SAUCE

In typical "Texas barbecue," the sauce is served on the side—for dipping ribs, for spooning on each bite. The sauce is also tossed with shredded beef or pork, and heaped onto grill-toasted buns for great sandwiches in true Texas fashion.
Makes 3 cups (750 mL).

1/4 pound (125 grams)	butter
1/3 cup (75 mL)	corn oil
1 medium-sized	onion, peeled and minced
4 stalks	celery, finely chopped
1 small	green pepper, stemmed, seeded and finely chopped
2 cloves	garlic, peeled and minced
2/3 cup (150 mL)	tomato catsup
2/3 cup (150 mL)	tomato-based chili sauce
2/3 cup (150 mL)	apple cider vinegar
3 tbsp. (45 mL)	molasses
1/3 cup (75 mL)	Worcestershire sauce
12-ounce (375-mL) can	beer, room-temperature *or* water
2	bay leaves, crumbled
1/2 tsp. (2 mL)	liquid smoke flavoring
1 tbsp. (15 mL)	chili powder
2 tsp. (10 mL)	coarsely ground black pepper
	salt, to taste

Melt butter in a very large cast-iron skillet or a large saucepan. Add the oil and heat until bubbly. Stir in the onions, celery and green pepper. Sauté, stirring, over medium-high heat until vegetables are softened and pale golden in color, about 15 minutes.

Stir in the remaining ingredients, whisking until smooth and thoroughly combined. Bring mixture to a simmer, reduce heat to low, and cook sauce, partially covered, 25–30 minutes to blend flavors. Taste and correct for salt and seasonings, and remove sauce from heat. Cool to room temperature, cover tightly in glass jars and refrigerate until ready to use.

Serve sauce barely warm or room-temperature for dipping. If tossing with shredded, cooked beef or pork, serve warmed.

FLORIDA BARBECUE SAUCE

This wonderful sauce is often encountered at southern barbecues in Jackson-ville, Georgia, Alabama—or even Miami! This sauce with its fresh lemon, butter and horseradish flavor is a sure-fire winner. **Makes 3 cups (750 mL).**

1/2 pound (250 grams)	butter
1 whole	lemon, ground (including rind)
1 whole	lime, ground (including rind)
3 tbsp. (45 mL)	fresh lemon juice
1/2 cup (125 mL)	prepared horseradish
4 tbsp. (60 mL)	brown sugar, packed
1/2 cup (125 mL)	bottled chili sauce (the type used for shrimp cocktails and hamburgers)
1/3 cup (75 mL)	apple cider vinegar
10 drops	liquid hot-pepper sauce (Tabasco)
pinch	ground cloves
1/2 tsp. (2 mL)	salt

In a deep, stainless steel saucepan, melt the butter over low heat. Add the remaining ingredients and bring mixture to a slow simmer. Cook 30–35 minutes, stirring occasionally. Cool sauce completely. Cover tightly and refrigerate until ready to use. Bring to room temperature, or gently reheat, before using or serving.

CALIFORNIA CITRUS BARBECUE SAUCE

This tangy, refreshing sauce is typically Californian, with the flavor of both fresh oranges and lemons. It teams beautifully with poultry, fish and ribs.
Makes 4 cups (1 litre).

2 cups (500 mL)	tomato purée
3/4 cup (175 mL)	catsup
1 medium	onion, peeled and finely minced or ground
2 large cloves	garlic, peeled and minced
1 large	orange, ground (entire orange, including peel)
1 large	lemon, ground (entire lemon, including rind)
1/2 cup (125 mL)	brown sugar, packed
1/3 cup (75 mL)	apple cider vinegar
1 tbsp. (15 mL)	chili powder
1/2 tsp. (2 mL)	ground cinnamon
1/2 tsp. (2 mL)	ground allspice
1/2 tsp. (2 mL)	liquid smoke

Combine all ingredients in a deep, stainless steel sauce pan over low heat, and bring to a simmer. Simmer barbecue sauce 20 minutes, stirring occasionally. Remove sauce from heat and cool.

Note: This sauce is best prepared 24 hours ahead of use for best flavor. Sauce may be stored in refrigerator, covered, up to one week.

"BEST-EVER" BARBECUE SAUCE

This sauce is delicious and simple to make, as it relies on many prepared products from your pantry. Prepare sauce 1–3 days in advance and keep refrigerated until ready to use. This one may just become one of your "home-made" standards. Sauce may be kept refrigerated in glass jars, tightly capped, 6–8 weeks. **Makes 2 quarts (2 litres) sauce.**

4 tbsp. (60 mL)	butter
4 tbsp. (60 mL)	vegetable oil
1 large	onion, peeled and finely diced
18-ounce (550 mL) jar	best-quality, hickory-flavored barbecue sauce, hot or mild
10-ounce (300 mL) jar	bitter-orange marmalade
1 small	orange, ground (including rind)
1	lemon, ground (including rind)
4 tbsp. (60 mL)	Worcestershire sauce
12-ounce (375 mL)	chutney
1/3 cup (75 mL)	molasses
1/2 tsp. (2 mL)	liquid smoke flavoring
	salt
1 tsp. (5 mL)	cracked black peppercorns

In a deep, stainless steel saucepan, heat the butter and oil over medium heat until butter foams. Add the onions and sauté, stirring, until softened and pale golden in color. Stir in all remaining ingredients and bring mixture to a simmer. Cook, stirring, until marmalade melts and ingredients are completely blended. Reduce heat to low, and cook sauce partially covered until thickened, glossy and flavors are well blended—about 40 minutes. Stir occasionally.

Remove sauce from heat. Cool completely. Transfer sauce to clean glass jars, cap tightly and refrigerate until ready to use.

APRICOT BARBECUE SAUCE

This fruity barbecue sauce is great to use with pork ribs, chicken, game hens or duck. Brush over meats during final 15 minutes of grilling time, so that sauce will not burn. **Makes 3 cups (750 mL) sauce.**

3 tbsp. (45 mL)	oil
1 medium	onion, peeled and minced
2 cloves	garlic, peeled and minced
16-ounce (450-mL)	apricot preserves
3 tbsp. (45 mL)	cider vinegar
2 tbsp. (30 mL)	Worcestershire sauce
3 tbsp. (45 mL)	Bourbon or Scotch whiskey
pinch	ground allspice
pinch	ground cinnamon
10 drops	liquid hot-pepper sauce (Tabasco)
4 tbsp. (60 mL)	butter

Heat the oil in a deep, stainless steel saucepan over medium heat. Add the minced onion and sauté 5–6 minutes until softened and pale golden in color. Stir in the garlic and sauté 2 minutes. Add the apricot preserves, vinegar, Worcestershire, Bourbon, allspice, cinnamon and hot-pepper sauce. Bring mixture to a simmer, reduce heat to low and cook 15 minutes, stirring. Finally, stir in the butter until melted and bubbly. Remove sauce from heat, and set aside to cool to room temperature before using.

Sauce may be prepared several days ahead of time, capped tightly and refrigerated. Bring to room temperature and reheat gently before using.

Opposite: Apricot-Glazed Baby Back Ribs, Deviled Barbecued Beef Ribs.

BREAKFAST BASTING SAUCE

This is a wonderful, very simple sauce to baste sausages, ham, bacon slices and tender pork riblets for breakfast or brunch. It also serves as a baste for grilled potatoes and fruits. **Makes 3 cups (750 mL).**

1/2 pound (150 grams)	butter
1 cup (250 mL)	apple cider vinegar
1 tsp. (5 mL)	salt
2 tbsp. (30 mL)	molasses
1 tbsp. (15 mL)	Worcestershire sauce
2 tbsp. (30 mL)	tomato catsup
1/3 cup (75 mL)	vegetable oil
6 drops	liquid hot-pepper seasoning (Tabasco)

Melt butter in a heavy saucepan until butter foams. Stir in the vinegar, salt, molasses, Worcestershire sauce, catsup and oil. Whisk until smooth. Bring mixture to a simmer over low heat and cook 2 minutes. Season with Tabasco.

Remove sauce from heat. Cool completely, and store, refrigerated, until ready to use. Bring sauce to room temperature and reheat gently to warm before using.

PORK RUB DRY SEASONING MIX

This is a dry seasoning "marinade"—one to rub over any cut of pork, especially slab spareribs, country-style ribs, and baby back ribs. This is the "rub" that gets the ball rolling on the grill. Then during the final stages of barbecuing— brush with your favorite barbecue sauce. **Makes 1/2 cup (125 mL).**

2 tbsp. (30 mL)	salt
2 tbsp. (30 mL)	sugar
1 tbsp. (15 mL)	finely grated lemon rind
1 tbsp. (15 mL)	finely grated orange rind
1 tbsp. (15 mL)	paprika
1 tbsp. (15 mL)	freshly ground black pepper
1 tbsp. (15 mL)	ground coriander
1 tsp. (5 mL)	dry mustard

Whisk all ingredients together in a small bowl until thoroughly blended. Store in a small jar, refrigerated. To use, rub onto all surfaces of pork before grilling. Allow to set 30 minutes before barbecuing.

MAPLE SYRUP GLAZE

This wonderful glaze has a base of pure maple syrup, butter, fresh lemon juice and a shot of Bourbon for kick. Use to baste split game hens, chicken, pork loin, Canadian bacon, ham steaks and tender, pork baby back ribs.
Makes 1 1/2 cups (375 mL).

1 1/2 cups (375 mL)	pure maple syrup
3 tbsp. (45 mL)	fresh lemon juice
1 tsp. (5 mL)	finely grated lemon rind
3 tbsp. (45 mL)	Bourbon
1/4 pound (125 grams)	butter, chilled and cut into 8 pieces
	pinch salt

Heat the maple syrup in a small, heavy saucepan until reduced by half, to 3/4 cup (175 mL), and thickened. Stir in the lemon juice, rind and Bourbon, and simmer 3–4 minutes until bubbly. Reduce heat to very low and whisk in the cold butter, one piece at a time. Add each additional piece butter when previous one has just melted into mixture. Add a pinch of salt, whisk smooth and remove from heat. Set aside until ready to use.

SPICY CRANBERRY GLAZE

For years, there was a popular "word of mouth" barbecue sauce going around between cooks that combined a jar of grape jelly and a jar of chili sauce. That was it! And it was good—but this one's better. Cranberry sauce, the same chili sauce, and some added flavorings make this a great glaze for turkey, chicken, duck and ribs. **Makes 3 1/2 cups (875 mL) sauce.**

4 tbsp. (60 mL)	corn oil
1/3 cup (75 mL)	finely minced onion
1-pound (500-gram) can	whole cranberry sauce, puréed
1 12-ounce (375 mL) bottle	chili sauce (tomato-based, for hamburgers)
2 tbsp. (30 mL)	fresh lime juice
2 tsp. (10mL)	finely grated lime peel (green part only)
1/4 tsp. (1 mL)	cayenne pepper
10 drops	liquid hot-pepper sauce (Tabasco)
1/2 tsp. (2 mL)	coarsely ground black pepper
1/2 tsp. (2 mL)	ground allspice

Heat the oil in a saucepan over medium heat and add the minced onion. Sauté 3–4 minutes, stirring, until onions are softened. Add remaining ingredients and bring mixture to a simmer. Simmer 3 minutes. Remove from heat and cool. Transfer to glass jars with tight-fitting lids, and refrigerate until ready to use. Bring to room temperature, or gently reheat before using.

NEW ORLEANS CREOLE SAUCE

This is the authentic New Orleans creole sauce. It is delicious with any seafood done on the grill and adds a savory smack to a combination of barbecued chicken and smoked sausages. **Makes generous 3 cups (750 mL).**

2 tbsp. (30 mL)	butter
2 tbsp. (30 mL)	bacon drippings
2 large cloves	garlic, peeled and crushed
2/3 cup (150 mL)	*each* finely diced onion, celery, green onion and green bell pepper
1 tbsp. (15 mL)	sugar
1 tsp. (5 mL)	paprika
2	bay leaves
3 cups (750 mL)	crushed canned tomatoes
2 tsp (10 mL)	red wine vinegar
1 tsp. (5 mL)	thyme leaves
	salt
	freshly ground black pepper

Heat the butter and bacon drippings in a deep, stainless steel saucepan over medium-high heat. Add the garlic and sauté 2–3 minutes until softened. Stir in the diced onion, celery, green onion and bell pepper. Sauté until vegetables are softened and just turn pale golden. Stir in the sugar, paprika and bay leaves and cook 3 minutes. Add the tomatoes, vinegar and thyme and bring mixture to a simmer. Reduce heat to low and simmer sauce for 1 hour. Stir occasionally until glossy and thickened. Season to taste with salt and pepper.

Cool sauce completely. Store, covered, in refrigerator up to three days before serving. Serve sauce warm, not hot, for best flavor.

AÏOLI

Aïoli sauce is a pungent, garlic-spiked mayonnaise. Wildly popular along the French Riviera, it is served with a basket of fresh crudités (sliced raw vegetables) for dipping. This wonderful sauce makes a great accompaniment to grilled shellfish such as scallops, shrimp, crabmeat and lobster, as well as an assortment of grilled fresh vegetables. Makes 1 1/2 cups (375 grams).

4 fresh cloves	garlic, peeled and quartered
1 tsp. (5 mL)	salt
2	egg yolks at room temperature
1 1/4 cups (300 mL)	olive oil
1 tbsp. (15 mL)	fresh lemon juice
1 tbsp. (15 mL)	Dijon mustard

In a food processor, purée the garlic and salt to a fine paste, scraping down sides with a rubber scraper. Add the egg yolks and beat until very creamy and frothy. With the motor running, add the olive oil in a very thin, slow, steady stream—beginning with a few drops. Finally, add the lemon juice and mustard and beat in until smooth.

Store finished aïoli in a glass jar, tightly covered, for up to 5 days. Whisk smooth before serving. Serve chilled or cool.

FRESH BASIL AÏOLI

This fresh, basil-flecked, lovely green aïoli is delicious slathered over a sizzling piece of succulent grilled fish or chicken, hot off the coals. It is also wonderful on hot corn on the cob, or charcoal-grilled beefsteak tomatoes. Makes 1 1/2 cups (375 grams).

3 fresh cloves	garlic, peeled and quartered
1 tsp. (5 mL)	salt
1/2 cup (125 mL)	fresh basil leaves, packed
2	egg yolks, room temperaure
3/4 cup (175 mL)	olive oil
1/2 cup (125 mL)	safflower oil
1 tbsp. (15 mL)	fresh lemon juice
1 tbsp. (15 mL)	fresh lemon rind (yellow part only)
	freshly ground black pepper

In a food processor, purée the garlic and salt to a fine paste, scraping down sides with a rubber scraper. Add the basil leaves and process to a fine purée. Add the egg yolks and continue to process until smooth and completely incorporated. With the motor running, add the olive oil in a very thin, slow, steady stream—beginning with a few drops. Continue with the safflower oil. Finally, add the lemon juice and rind and beat until smooth. Season to taste with pepper.

Store finished aïoli in a glass jar, tightly covered, for up to 5 days. Whisk smooth before serving. Serve chilled or cool.

FRESH BASIL PESTO SAUCE

Fresh basil pesto is great to keep on hand, as it makes a wonderful accompaniment to grilled fish, poultry, steaks, chops, roasted potatoes and corn. It is wonderful with barbecue veal chops or a chicken breast.
Makes generous 2 cups (500 mL).

3 large cloves	garlic, peeled and quartered
1 tsp. (5 mL)	salt
2 cups (500 mL)	fresh basil leaves, packed
1/2 cup (125 mL)	fresh parsley leaves, packed
1/2 cup (125 mL)	pine nuts, toasted 8–10 minutes in a 325° F. (160° C.) oven
2/3 cup (150 mL)	freshly grated Parmesan cheese
1 cup (250 mL)	olive oil

In a food processor, purée the garlic and salt to a paste, scraping sides down with a rubber scraper. Add the fresh basil and parsley, and continue to process to a fine paste. Add the pine nuts and process until smooth. Add the cheese. With the motor running, add the olive oil in a very thin, slow, steady stream until incorporated. Finished pesto sauce should be the consistency of grainy mayonnaise. Transfer finished sauce to a glass jar with a tight-fitting lid. Cover sauce with a thin film of olive oil, cap, and refrigerate until ready to use. Bring to room temperature 15 minutes before serving.

HOMEMADE TARTARE SAUCE

Making your own tartare sauce is simple and it is fresh tasting and utterly delicious. Prepare this sauce several hours before serving, or the night before, and serve with grilled halibut, albacore, catfish, sea bass or salmon. Makes 1 1/2 cups (375 mL).

1/2 cup (125 mL) *each*	mayonnaise and sour cream
1/3 cup (75 mL)	sweet pickle relish, completely drained
1 tbsp. (15 mL)	tiny capers, drained
2 tbsp. (30 mL)	finely minced or grated onion
8 drops	liquid hot-pepper sauce (Tabasco)
1/2 tsp. (2 mL)	*each* salt and freshly ground black pepper
1 tbsp. (15 mL)	very finely minced parsley
1 tsp. (5 mL)	fresh lemon juice
2 tsp. (10 mL)	finely grated lemon rind
	pinch cayenne pepper

Combine all ingredients in a small mixing bowl and whisk together. Cover tightly and chill several hours or overnight before serving.

SPICY SZECHWAN SAUCE

This is a wonderful, spicy, Oriental-inspired sauce. It is especially suited to shrimp, swordfish, snapper and baby back pork ribs.
Makes 1 1/2 cups (375 mL).

4 tbsp. (60 mL)	peanut oil
2 tbsp. (30 mL)	Oriental sesame oil
2/3 cup (150 mL)	minced scallions (6 scallions)
2 large cloves	garlic, peeled and minced
2 tbsp. (30 mL)	minced fresh ginger
3 dried	red chili peppers, broken in small pieces
1/3 cup (75 mL)	soy sauce
2 tbsp. (30 mL)	Sherry
1/4 cup (50 mL)	brown sugar, packed
2 tbsp. (30 mL)	Sherry wine vinegar
1/3 cup (75 mL)	tomato catsup
2 tbsp. (30 mL)	water

Heat the peanut oil and sesame oil in a wok or medium-sized saucepan over medium-high heat. Add the scallions, garlic, ginger and crumbled chili peppers and stir-fry 2–3 minutes. Reduce heat to medium and stir in the remaining ingredients. Simmer sauce 5 minutes, stirring, and cool.

MEATS ON THE GRILL

Let's get to the meat of the matter. What is more mouth-watering than smoky, meaty ribs, glazed to perfection with a savory sauce? Perhaps a thick, prime beefsteak, done rare, with a perfectly charred exterior slathered with garlic butter. Or skewers of lamb shish kebab, marinated in olive oil and herbs, done to a rosy turn over hot coals. Maybe thick veal chops, grilled to a juicy finish, topped with a spicy green-chili butter. This chapter is filled with recipes for hearty food for meat lovers—the perfect burger, with "the works," spicy "jerked" ribs from Jamaica, racks of Provençal-style lamb done on the grill, even a breakfast barbecue! So whatever your fancy—be it beef, pork, lamb, veal or ribs—it's all here. Come and get it!

FLORENTINE GRILLED T-BONE STEAKS

The Florentines are masters at grilling steaks and enjoy them with great gusto. Rubbed with very fruity olive oil and rosemary before grilling, they are superb. Serve, Italian-style, with mounds of fresh green beans, oven-roasted potatoes in olive oil and garlic, and with wedges of fresh lemon to squeeze over the steaks. Serves 4.

4	T-bone steaks, cut 1 1/2" (4 cm) thick
1/2 cup (125 mL)	extra-virgin olive oil
4 tbsp. (60 mL)	rosemary leaves
1 bunch	additional fresh rosemary, soaked in warm water 30 minutes and drained
	salt
	coarse-ground black peppercorns
	additional cruet of olive oil
	fresh lemon wedge

Brush steaks on both sides with olive oil and sprinkle each with 1 tbsp. (15 mL) rosemary leaves. Allow steaks to sit at room temperature 45 minutes while preparing coals.

Heat coals to medium-hot, about 45 minutes to 1 hour. Lightly oil grill. Place drained bunch of rosemary, separated into sprigs, directly on hot coals. Place steaks on grill and cook approximately 4–6 inches (10–15 cm) from source of heat, about 5 minutes on each side for medium-rare. Steaks should be nicely charred on the outside and juicy and rosy-pink inside (meat should feel *just* slightly firmed when pressed). Season steaks with salt and pepper during final 2 minutes of grilling.

Remove steaks from the grill and serve on warmed plates. Pass a cruet of olive oil to drizzle over each steak, and accompany with fresh lemon wedges.

GINGERED HONEY BARBECUED FLANK STEAK

Flank steak is one of the great cuts of beef for the barbecue. It teams beautifully with marinades, grills evenly and when sliced on the diagonal across the grain, makes for a handsome presentation. Serve this steak with grilled fresh corn on the cob, smoky black beans, steamed white rice and a fresh beefsteak and red onion salad. Ice-cold beer is the perfect beverage. Serves 4.

1 2-pound (1 kg)	flank steak
2/3 cup (150 mL)	vegetable oil
1/3 cup (75 mL)	soy sauce
2 tbsp. (30 mL)	fresh orange juice
2 tbsp. (30 mL)	grated fresh ginger
2 large cloves	garlic, peeled and pressed
4 tbsp. (60 mL)	honey
4 tbsp. (60 mL)	Sherry wine vinegar
2	scallions, trimmed and finely mined
8 large	thick scallions (green onions)

Place flank steak in a rectangular glass baking dish just large enough to accommodate it. Whisk together the oil, soy sauce, orange juice, ginger, garlic, honey, vinegar and scallions. Pour half over steak, turn meat and cover with remainder of marinade. Cover and refrigerate steak 2–4 hours, turning meat 2–3 times. Bring to room temperature 20 minutes before grilling.

Lightly oil grill. Place steak over hot coals, 4" (10 cm) from source of heat. Grill 5 minutes per side for medium rare (meat should just yield when pressed). While steak is grilling, place whole scallions in marinade, turning. Remove meat from grill and allow to stand on cutting board 5 minutes before slicing.

While meat is resting, prepare grilled scallions. Place marinated scallions on hot, oiled grill and cook 2–3 minutes until lightly charred, turning once. Slice steak across the grain, on the diagonal, into thin strips. Season with salt and pepper. Serve with the hot, grilled scallions.

GRILLED PROVENÇAL BEEF FILET

Beef doesn't get any better than this! A whole prime beef filet done over hickory, with a marinade of dried herbes de provençe, red wine and olive oil. Grill rare or medium-rare, and serve with garlicky mashed potatoes enriched with cream, fresh haricot verts (thin French green beans) and grilled whole mushrooms.
Serves 6-8.

1 whole	prime beef filet, about 4 1/2 pounds (2250 grams)
1/2 cup (125 mL)	olive oil
1/3 cup (75 mL)	dry red wine
3 large cloves	garlic, peeled and pressed
3 tbsp. (45 mL)	dried herbes de provençe (thyme, basil, savory, fennel and lavender)
2 tsp. (10 mL)	cracked black peppercorns
2 tbsp. (30 mL)	minced fresh shallots
2 cups (500 mL)	hickory chips, soaked 30 minutes in warm water, drained assorted grilled mushrooms (optional) sprigs of fresh rosemary and thyme, as garnish

Select a prime beef filet. Tuck under the thinner "tail-end" and tie with string to close. Whisk together the olive oil, red wine, garlic, herbs, pepper and shallots. Pour marinade over filet, turn to coat, and let stand at room temperature 2 hours. Turn meat several times.

Prepare coals to medium-hot, about 45 minutes. Scatter drained hickory chips over coals. Place grill 4" (10 cm) above heat. Oil grill.

Remove meat from marinade and place on grill. Sear on all sides, turning, about 12 minutes until crusty. Move filet to edges of grill where heat is not so intense, continue to grill until medium-rare, about 20–24 minutes longer. Internal temperature should be about 145° F. (65° C.).

Remove filet from grill and allow to rest 10 minutes before slicing. Serve, if desired, with hot, grilled, fresh mushrooms, and garnish with sprigs of fresh herbs.

To make the assorted grilled mushrooms, select from tightly closed button mushrooms, fresh shitaki and fresh clusters of oyster mushrooms.

Wipe mushrooms clean with a damp cloth. Do not soak or rinse in water. Brush with olive oil and place on grill. Cook several minutes on each side until golden brown, brushing with oil. Do not overcook mushrooms—they should be lightly grilled, tender and should not shrink in size. Season lightly with salt and pepper during final 1 minute on grill. Serve hot.

Leftover marinade can be used as a sauce. Reduce in a small sauce-pan until glossy and syrupy, remove from heat and whisk in several table-spoons (30–60 mL) of cold butter. Serve over slices of beef.

GRILLED BEEF FILETS BOUND IN BACON WITH GORGONZOLA BUTTER

If done properly, thick tenderloin filets are marvelous cooked on the grill. Wrap each filet in a strip of smoky bacon, and top with a generous chunk of chilled Gorgonzola Butter. **Serves 4.**

4 1 1/2"-2" (4 cm-5 cm)	thick beefsteak filets (tenderloin steaks)
4 thick-sliced slices	smoked bacon, blanched 30 seconds in simmering water and drained
4 tbsp. (60 mL)	bacon drippings
	salt
	cracked black peppercorns
1 recipe	Gorgonzola Butter (page 28)

Prepare coals to medium-hot, about 45 minutes. Wrap each filet in the blanched bacon and tie with string to fasten. Bring steaks to room temperature, about 25 minutes.

Oil grill, or brush with bacon drippings. Brush one side of each steak with bacon drippings and place, oiled side down, on grill. Sear 1 minute. Brush other side with drippings, and turn to sear. Season with salt and black peppercorns and continue to grill steaks to medium-rare—about 5–6 minutes per side. Steaks should just begin to feel very slightly firmed when pressed.

Remove steaks from grill, and snip string and discard. Top each steak with a generous piece of chilled Gorgonzola Butter, and serve piping hot.

TEXAS BARBECUED BRISKET OF BEEF

A brisket of beef is marvelous done on the grill, and the leftovers (if there are any!) make wonderful sandwiches on butter-toasted buns. This is one of those rare times I suggest a commercial meat tenderizer, as brisket is normally cooked slow and long. Serve with hot cornbread, potato salad, cole slaw and baked beans—with ice-cold beer for a true Texas barbecue. **Serves 8–10.**

4-5 pound (2-2 1/2 kg)	beef brisket
1/3 cup (75 mL)	cider vinegar
1/4 cup (50 mL)	corn oil
2 tbsp. (30 mL)	chili powder
2 tbsp. (30 mL)	Worcestershire sauce
1/2 tsp. (2 mL)	black pepper
2 cloves	garlic, peeled and minced
12-ounce (375 mL) can	beer at room temperature
2 tbsp. (30 mL)	tomato catsup
	unseasoned meat tenderizer
1 recipe	Real Texas Barbecue Sauce (page 30)

Whisk together the vinegar, corn oil, chili powder, Worcestershire, black pepper, garlic, beer and catsup. Place brisket in a shallow bowl or heavy-duty plastic bag. Pour marinade over brisket, turning to coat evenly. Refrigerate 6 hours, or overnight, until ready to barbecue. Bring meat to room temperature while preparing coals.

When the coals are ashen white, about 1 hour, separate and spread out to form a single layer. Place grill 4"–6" (10–15 cm) above hot coals. Oil grill.

Remove brisket from marinade, allowing excess to drip off. Sprinkle both sides of meat with tenderizer and allow to sit 5 minutes. Place beef on grill and cook until medium—about 150° F. (65° C.) on a meat thermometer. If medium-rare is desired, cook to 135–140° F. (60° C.). Turn meat frequently during cooking, brushing with marinade.

Heat Real Texas Barbecue Sauce to just warm, basting over meat during final 2–3 minutes of cooking, if desired.

Remove meat from grill and place on a wooden carving board to rest 10 minutes before serving. Carve meat across the grain into thin, slanted slices. Serve generous portions, accompanied by the sauce on the side.

KOREAN BEEF SHORT RIBS ON THE GRILL

The Korean style of short ribs on the grill is hard to beat. Marinated in a pungent combination of soy sauce, scallions, garlic and sesame, they are perfected with the flavor of charcoal. Serve these hearty ribs with steamed rice, a raw cabbage salad and crisp, steamed asparagus. **Serves 4–6.**

6 pounds (3 kg)	thick, beef short ribs, cut into 4" (10 cm) lengths
1/2 cup (125 mL)	soy sauce
1/2 cup (125 mL)	dry red wine
4 tbsp. (60 mL)	dark brown sugar, packed
4 large cloves	garlic, peeled and pressed
1/2 cup (125 mL)	minced green scallions
1/3 cup (75 mL)	Oriental sesame oil
1/3 cup (75 mL)	toasted sesame seeds
1 tsp. (5 mL)	cracked black peppercorns
2 tbsp. (30 mL)	minced fresh ginger
	minced scallions, as garnish

Toast the sesame seeds in a small skillet over medium heat 3 minutes, stirring, until golden brown. Set aside to cool.

In a food processor or blender, combine the soy sauce, red wine, sugar, garlic, scallions, sesame oil, toasted sesame seeds, pepper and ginger. Whirl until completely blended.

Place ribs on cutting board with bone side down. Slash meaty part on top in a "criss-cross" pattern 1/2" (1 cm) wide x 1/2" (1 cm) deep. Place ribs and marinade in a heavy-duty plastic bag, close tightly and place in a shallow dish. Refrigerate ribs and marinate 6–8 hours, or overnight, turning bag several times.

Bring ribs to room temperature while preparing coals. Prepare coals to ashen white, about 1 hour. Oil grill and set 4"–6" (10 cm–15 cm) above source of heat.

Remove ribs from marinade, and place on grill. Barbecue, turning and basting frequently with marinade until ribs are tender and well browned on all sides, with crisped edges. Cooking time will be about 30 minutes for medium-rare.

Transfer ribs to a large wooden platter and sprinkle with minced scallions.

DEVILED BARBECUED BEEF RIBS

Big, meaty, "dinosaur-sized," beef rib bones are great fun to eat. Kids adore them and when done over hickory, they are at their best. Grill with any favorite barbecue sauce, or try these, with a "deviled" mustard sauce. **Serves 4.**

12 large	beef rib bones (from the prime rib)
2	lemons, halved
	salt and lemon-pepper
2 cups (500 mL)	hickory chips, soaked 30 minutes in warm water, drained
1 recipe	Deviled Mustard Glaze (recipe follows)

Bring ribs to room temperature, rub with cut lemons on both sides, and season liberally with salt and lemon-pepper. Prepare coals to medium-hot, about 45 minutes. Spread coals out in an even layer. Scatter soaked and drained hickory chips evenly over coals. Oil grill and place 4" (10 cm) above hot coals.

Place ribs, rounded side down, on grill and brown one side. Turn and brown other side. Brush browned ribs very lightly with Deviled Mustard Glaze, and continue to cook until ribs are tender and crusty. Total cooking time will be about 12–15 minutes. Brush with glaze again during final 3–4 minutes cooking time to glaze ribs.

Deviled Mustard Glaze

6 tbsp. (90 mL)	butter
2 tbsp. (30 mL)	vegetable oil *or* olive oil
1/3 cup (75 mL)	finely minced scallions (white and green part)
3 cloves	garlic, peeled and minced
4 tbsp. (60 mL)	Worcestershire sauce
2 tbsp. (30 mL)	fresh lemon juice
1/4 cup (50 mL)	Dijon mustard
1/3 cup (75 mL)	grainy mustard
1/4 tbsp. (1 mL)	cayenne pepper
5–6 drops	liquid hot-pepper sauce (Tabasco)

Heat butter and oil in a skillet until butter foams. Add the minced scallions and sauté 3–4 minutes until just softened. Stir in the garlic and sauté 1–2 minutes. Stir in the Worcestershire sauce and lemon juice, and heat sauce until bubbly. Remove skillet from heat. Whisk in the two mustards, cayenne and Tabasco. Set aside until ready to use.

THE PERFECTIONIST'S STEAK

*This is the ultimate steak, cooked to perfection, the natural juices sealed inside a crusty exterior with a faint flavor of smoke. Serve, if desired, with a chilled pat of any of the savory butters in this book. The perfect accompaniments: baked or roasted potatoes, grilled onions, tossed green salad, crusty garlic bread and a bottle of dry red wine. **Serves 4.***

4 thick	prime beefsteaks: New York strip, club, Spencer steak, T-bone, porterhouse, sirloin; each cut 1 1/2"–2" (4 cm–5 cm) thick
	salt
	coarsely ground black pepper
1 recipe	savory butter (see "Marinades, Flavored Butters, Sauces and Glazes") for a selection)
	mesquite or other hot-burning charcoal

Bring steaks to room temperature while preparing coals to hot, about 1 hour. Place grill 4" (10 cm) above heat, and oil grill.

Place steaks on grill and sear 7 minutes, or until natural juices begin to bubble up through surface of meat. Using tongs (do not pierce meat), turn steak and sear other side, cooking until bubbles appear.

Continue to grill to rare or medium-rare; total cooking time will be about 14–15 minutes for a very thick steak; less for a thinner one. When pressed with finger, meat should just begin to feel a bit resistant. Season with salt and pepper during final 1 minute.

Remove steaks from grill and allow to rest 3–4 minutes before serving for meat to absorb all its juices. Top each steak, if desired, with a generous pat of chilled savory butter. (Suggested butters are: Fresh Basil Mustard Butter (page 24), Gorgonzola Butter (page 28), Kräuter Butter (Fresh Herbed Butter) (page 20), Garlic and Herbed Lemon Butter (page 21).

BURGERS WITH "THE WORKS"

These great grilled burgers have it all—cheese, onion, olives, green pepper—right in the beef! All they need is a buttered, whole-wheat bun, grilled until toasted over hot coals, a thick slice of beefsteak tomato and a ruffle of lettuce. Serve with ice-cold milk or beer, or old-fashioned lemonade. **Makes 4 generous burgers.**

1 1/2 pounds (750 grams)	ground chuck (not too lean)
3 slices	smoked bacon, ground (a food processor does the trick)
1 cup (250 mL)	coarsely grated sharp Cheddar cheese
1/2 cup (125 mL)	*each* finely diced onion, black ripe olives, green bell pepper
1 tbsp (15 mL)	dried oregano
1 tsp. (5 mL)	*each* salt and black pepper
4 large	sesame-topped whole-wheat buns, split and buttered
	sliced tomatoes
	lettuce leaves
	mayonnaise, chili sauce, Dijon mustard

Combine the ground beef, bacon, cheese, onion, olives, green bell pepper, oregano, salt and pepper. Knead gently but thoroughly for several minutes until well mixed and mixture binds together. Form into 4 thick, round patties. Refrigerate 1–2 hours to blend flavors.

Prepare coals to medium-hot, about 45 minutes. Place grill 3"–4" (7 cm–10 cm) above coals. Oil grill. Place burgers on grill and sear 6 minutes. Using a wide metal spatula, turn burgers and grill additional 5–6 minutes for rare, additional 7–8 minutes for medium rare. Outside of burgers should be a crusty, golden brown.

Remove burgers and allow to rest 2–3 minutes while toasting buns. Place buttered side of buns down, on outer edges of grill, and toast until a rich, golden brown. Watch carefully, so that buns do not burn.

Serve burgers on toasted buns and pass the condiments.

Opposite: Florentine Grilled T-Bone Steak.

HERB GRILLED PORK CHOPS

Try these tantalizing, aromatic pork chops on the grill and—I guarantee it—no others will be quite as good. Perfumed with olive oil and fresh sage leaves, these thick chops are slightly charred on the outside and juicy and succulent inside. Serve with a risotto with fresh mushrooms, a crisp green salad and grilled vegetables. **Serves 4.**

4	pork loin or rib chops, 1 1/4" (3 cm) thick
1/2 cup (125 mL)	olive oil
1 large clove	garlic, peeled and pressed
1 tbsp. (15 mL)	fresh lemon juice
	salt and coarsely ground black peppercorns
16	fresh sage leaves
	additional bunch fresh sage leaves

Combine the olive oil, garlic and lemon juice. Brush over pork chops, both sides. Season with salt and pepper. Press 2 fresh sage leaves on each side of each chop. Allow to stand 20 minutes.

Place additional bunch of sage leaves directly on bed of coals. Lightly oil grill, and place chops on grill 4"–6" (10 cm–15 cm) above coals. Grill, turning once or twice, until chops are well browned and slightly charred on the outside, juicy and *just* no longer pink on the inside, about 12–14 minutes total. When pressed with the finger, meat should just feel firmed. Remove from grill, allow chops to stand 5–8 minutes before serving.

APRICOT-GLAZED BABY BACK RIBS

Serve these succulent slabs of tender baby back ribs, one slab per person, and prepare for raves. Basted in a sticky, apricot-flavored sauce, these ribs have to be tasted to be believed. Serve with sharp knives for cutting into finger-sized ribs, and provide large checkered napkins to tuck under chins. **Serves 4.**

4 slabs	baby back pork ribs
1 large	orange, cut in half
1	lemon, cut in half
	salt
	freshly ground black pepper
2/3 cup (150 mL)	cider vinegar
1 recipe	Apricot Barbecue Sauce (page 34), slightly warmed

Bring ribs to room temperature. Rub both sides of each slab with orange and lemon juice. Allow to sit while preparing coals.

Prepare coals to medium-hot, about 45 minutes. Place grill 6" (15 cm) from source of heat. Oil grill. Place ribs on grill, thick side down. Sear 4 minutes, salt and pepper, and turn ribs. Sear on other side 4 minutes, and season with salt and pepper. Continue to grill ribs, basting with cider vinegar, 12–15 minutes per side.

Begin basting with Apricot Barbecue Sauce, and finish ribs on both sides 10–15 minutes. Ribs should be slightly charred and just tender. Remove ribs to warmed platters and allow to rest 10 minutes before serving.

SUNSHINE-STATE STICKY RIBS

Anyone who has ever been to the southern United States and had the good fortune to enjoy real southern barbecue has certainly run across a wonderful sauce called "Florida Barbecue Sauce." Lemony, buttery, with more than a dash of horseradish, this sauce is superb on ribs—especially the meaty, tender baby backs. **Serves 4.**

4 whole slabs	baby back ribs
2	lemons, cut in half
1 recipe	Florida Barbecue Sauce (page 31)
	salt
	freshly ground black pepper

Rub the baby back racks with lemon on both sides. Allow to sit at room temperature 20 minutes. Prepare coals to medium-hot, about 45 minutes. Lightly oil grill.

Place rib racks, meaty-side down, 4" (10 cm) from source of heat, and sear 5 minutes on *each* side. Season with salt and pepper. Begin basting with barbecue sauce, and continue to grill 15–18 minutes per side, turning slabs several times. Ribs should be sticky, highly glazed, nicely charred and just tender.

Remove ribs to a carving board, and let meat rest 8 minutes. Using a sharp knife, cut straight down between ribs to separate into 1- to 3-rib sections. Serve at once, accompanied by remainder of barbecue sauce for dipping.

JAMAICAN SPICY JERKED RIBS

In the past few years, Jamaican restaurants have sprung up in North America and, with them, a passionate following for their "jerked" meat—a unique method of barbecuing meat with a pungent seasoning rub. This is my version—Jamaican-style spareribs, coated with a spicy, fiery paste and grilled over bay-infused coals. Serve with a salad of fresh avocados, oranges and purple onion dressed in olive oil and fresh lime juice, hot steamed white rice and fresh wedges of lime-rubbed papaya and mango. The perfect accompaniment is ice-cold beer, and a lovely dessert is large scoops of fresh coconut ice cream.
Serves 6.

2 slabs	pork spareribs, 3–4 pounds each (1 1/2–2 kg), cut into 3-rib sections
2	limes, halved
2 large	onions, peeled and quartered
1	fresh lime, quartered
2 tsp. (10 mL)	salt
8 cloves	garlic, quartered
4	fresh or canned whole jalapeño peppers, stemmed and seeded
2 tbsp. (30 mL)	*each* ground ginger, allspice, cloves, chili powder, and dried oregano leaves
1 tbsp. (15 mL)	brown sugar
4 tbsp. (60 mL)	olive oil
18 whole	bay leaves, soaked in warm water 30 minutes and drained
	fresh avocado or citrus leaves, as garnish
	lime wedges

Cut a notch between each rib (top and bottom) 1/2" (1 cm) down on each three-rib section. Rub ribs with cut limes, and allow to sit in a single layer 10 minutes while preparing flavoring paste.

In a food processor, grind the onion and lime to a grainy paste. Add the salt and garlic and continue to process until paste-like. Add the peppers, ginger, allspice, cloves, chili powder, oregano and brown sugar, and process to combine. Finally, add the oil. Transfer paste to a small bowl.

Brush paste evenly over both sides or ribs and allow to stand 2 hours, spread out on butcher-paper in a single layer, before grilling.

Prepare coals to ashen white, about 1 hour. Spread coals out in a thin, even layer. Place grill 6" (15 cm) above coals. Scatter bay leaves over coals. Oil grill.

Place ribs, fat side up, on grill. Cook 5–6 minutes, turn and cook 5–6 minutes. If grill has a cover, place cover over ribs with damper opened. Continue to grill ribs, turning every 10 minutes, until tender and very crusty—about 1 hour.

Remove ribs from grill, and serve immediately on leaf-lined rustic platter or shallow wooden bowl. Garnish with fresh wedges of lime.

CALIFORNIA CITRUS-BARBECUED SPARERIBS

These ribs—with their tangy-sweet, fresh flavor of lemons and oranges—are sure to become a favorite. Serve with fresh corn, crusty garlic bread, a crisp green salad and smoky baked beans. Have lots of ice-cold beer on hand. **Serves 6.**

6–8 pounds (3–4 kg)	whole-slab pork spareribs
2	lemons, cut in half
	salt *or* garlic-seasoned salt
	freshly ground black pepper
1 recipe	California Citrus Barbecue Sauce (page 32)

Rub the spareribs on both sides with cut lemons. Allow to sit in a single layer at room temperature 20 minutes. Lightly oil grill, and prepare coals to medium-hot, about 1 hour.

Place ribs, meaty side down, 6" (15 cm) from coals and cook 15 minutes on *each* side *without* sauce, but seasoning lighting with salt and pepper. Baste ribs with sauce and cook additional 15 minutes on *each* side. Cook until tender, crusty brown and slightly charred. Remove ribs from grill. Keep barbecue sauce slightly warmed on side of grill.

Allow ribs to rest 15 minutes, then cut straight down between ribs to separate. Serve remainder of sauce with the ribs.

GRILLED SAUSAGE AND PEPPERS SANDWICHES

Anyone who has ever visited New York in the summertime and has had the good fortune to visit the frenzy of the San Gennaro festival in "little Italy" has most certainly savored the classic "sausage and peppers" sandwich. Make this perfect entertaining fare on a lazy summer day—offer both sweet and hot sausages, an array of colored peppers and grilled onions, and toast the very best Italian rolls you can find with garlic-flavored olive oil. **Serves 6–8.**

2 pounds (1 kg)	fresh Italian sausages, combination of both sweet (mild) and hot
6–8	Italian rolls, 6"–7" (15 cm–17 cm) long, *or* 2 long loaves Italian bread
3	green bell peppers, quartered
3	red bell peppers, quartered
2	yellow peppers, quartered
3	purple onions, peeled and sliced crosswise into thirds
1 1/2 cups (375 mL)	olive oil
3 large cloves	garlic, peeled and pressed
1 tbsp. (15 mL)	dried oregano leaves
4-5 drops	liquid hot-pepper seasoning (Tabasco)

Prepare coals to medium-hot, about 45 minutes. Place grill 4"–6" (10 cm–15 cm) above hot coals. Oil grill.

Gently prick sausages in several places with a thin skewer (to prevent sausages from bursting open during grilling). Bring sausages to room temperature, 20 minutes, before cooking. Whisk together the oil, garlic, oregano and Tabasco, and set aside.

Place sausages on grill. Brown on all sides, turning with tongs, for a total cooking time of 18–20 minutes. Place peppers and onions on outer perimeter of grill, brushing with flavored oil, and cook, turning, until golden brown and tender, with slightly crisped edges.

Slice open the rolls so that the two halves are opened, but still attached. Cut the loaves into three sections each, and split open each section just like the rolls. Brush cut sides generously with the flavored oil, and have ready to toast after sausages and peppers come off the grill.

Remove sausages, peppers and onions from grill. Place bread or rolls, oiled side down, on grill. Toast 1–3 minutes, watching very carefully, until golden brown. Remove from grill.

Serve each sandwich in parchment-lined shallow baskets, for fun. Into each sandwich place 2 sausages, several peppers and onions. Drizzle, if desired, with additional flavored oil. *Buon gusto!*

GRILLED RACKS OF LAMB PROVENÇAL

Rack of lamb seems high on everyone's list of favorites—and cooking them on an outside grill makes them a snap for entertaining. Cut lamb racks into 5-rib slabs, marinate overnight in this pungent Provençal-inspired mixture, and grill over rosemary-perfumed hot coals. Serve with grilled split zucchini, crookneck squash, and Japanese eggplant—all brushed with the same marinade. **Serves 6.**

6 individual racks	lamb, each 4–5 ribs wide
1 recipe	Provençal Marinade (page 15)
2 bunches	fresh rosemary, soaked 30 minutes in warm water and drained
	fresh sprigs rosemary, as garnish

Place individual racks of lamb in prepared Provençal Marinade, turn to coat and marinate at room temperature 2 hours.

Prepare coals to ashen white, about 1 hour. Place grill 4" (10 cm) above coals. Oil grill. Scatter drained rosemary sprigs directly on coals. Remove lamb from marinade and place on grill, thick side down. Sear lamb 5 minutes, turn and sear other side. Continue to grill lamb for a total cooking time of about 18 minutes, basting, until lamb is rosy-pink inside and very crusty outside. Inside temperature should register 140° F. (60–65° C.) for medium-rare.

Remove racks to a wooden board and allow to rest 8 minutes before serving for juices to be absorbed. Serve 1 rack per person, providing sharp steak knives for carving each rib into finger-held "chops." Garnish with sprigs of fresh rosemary, if desired.

BREAKFAST BARBECUE

On a lovely, sunshine-filled morning, when guests have stayed overnight and are anticipating the morning meal—nothing is nicer than breakfast done on the outdoor grill in the open air. With mugs of steaming coffee in hand, the morning air fills with the most appetizing aromas: smoky sausages, crisp bacon, succulent ham, apples and potatoes—all done over hot coals. Serve with a panful of Herbed Buttermilk Biscuits, a crock of butter and assorted preserves and honey, and a skillet of creamy scrambled eggs. **Serves 6.**

1 1/2 pounds (750 grams)	smoked, fully cooked sausage, such as kielbasa
12 slices	thick-sliced smoked bacon
2 slices, 3/4" (1.5 cm) thick	bone-in baked ham
3	apples, cored, cut into 1" (2 cm) rings
3 very large	russet potatoes, scrubbed, peel left intact; sliced lengthwise into 3/4" (1.5 cm) slices
1 recipe	Breakfast Basting Sauce (page 37)
1 dozen	eggs, scrambled in butter
1 recipe	Herbed Buttermilk Biscuits (page 153)
	assorted preserves, jams and honey
	crock of sweet butter
	fresh fruits or fresh-squeezed orange juice
	hot coffee

Prepare coals to ashen white, about 1 hour. Soak 2 cups applewood chips (if desired) in warm water 30 minutes, and drain. Prepare Breakfast Basting Sauce, and set aside.

Cut sausages into 5" (12 cm) lengths and either split open and lay flat, or slash on both sides in diagonal cuts.

Scatter drained chips on coals and place grill 6" (15 cm) over coals. Oil grill. Brush sausages, ham, apple rings, and sliced potatoes with basting sauce and place on grill. Place bacon slices on outer perimeter of grill.

Cook until sausages are a rich golden brown, basting with sauce and turning. Bacon will cook quickly; brush with basting sauce during final 1–2 minutes; cook until lightly crisped and golden brown. Cook ham slices, basting frequently, until just pale golden on both sides; do not overcook.

Grill apples and potatoes with basting sauce until golden brown and tender on both sides. Season with salt and pepper to taste.

Serve hot off the grill, with scrambled eggs, hot biscuits and all the suggested accompaniments.

GRILLED HERBED LOIN LAMB CHOPS

Nothing is better than prime lamb, with its naturally sweet flavor, over coals with a hint of fresh herbs. These are simple to prepare; serve with a great bottle of red wine, a gorgeous, mixed green salad and crisp, hot bread. Top with chilled slices of herb-flecked Kräuter Butter as the chops come off the grill. **Serves 4.**

8	loin lamb chops, each 1 1/2" (4 cm) thick
	olive oil
	dried thyme leaves or rosemary leaves (or combination of both)
	freshly ground black pepper and salt to taste
1 recipe	Kräuter Butter (page 20)
	lemon wedges
	sprigs of fresh rosemary and thyme, as garnish

Prepare coals to hot, about 1 hour. Place grill 3"–4" (7 cm–10 cm) above hot coals. Bring chops to room temperature and brush both sides with olive oil. Sprinkle generously with dried herbs. Allow chops to marinate while preparing coals.

Oil grill. Place chops on grill and sear 4 minutes per side. Continue to grill, brushing with additional olive oil as needed, until chops are a rich golden brown on either side and medium-rare inside; season to taste with salt and pepper during final 2–3 minutes cooking time. Total cooking time will be 14–18 minutes for a pink medium-rare. Do not overcook.

Remove chops from grill. Place a chilled slice or pat of Kräuter Butter on each sizzling chop, if desired. Garnish with lemon wedges and sprigs of fresh herbs. Serve at once.

BARBECUED BUTTERFLIED LEG OF LAMB "PROVENÇE"

A butterflied leg of lamb makes superb grilling. The thicker portions provide rosy-red slices, and the thinner sections provide crustier, medium-done slices. A quick marinade of olive oil and herbs with heady garlic provides the flavor— and the Fresh Basil Aïoli gives it the Provençal touch. Serve with grilled fresh vegetables, crusty French bread, a cool rice salad and a chilled French Rosé. Serves 6–8.

6-pound (3 kg)	leg of lamb, boned and butterflied
1/2 cup (75 mL)	olive oil
3 large cloves	fresh garlic, peeled and pressed
2 tbsp. (30 mL)	*each* dried thyme leaves and rosemary
1/3 cup (75 mL)	dry red wine
	salt and pepper
1 recipe	Fresh Basil Aïoli (page 40)
	grilled fresh vegetables
	large platter lined with bed of fresh thyme and rosemary sprigs

Press the butterflied leg of lamb out flat in a large, shallow dish. Brush with the olive oil, garlic, herbs and red wine on both sides. Turn to coat evenly. Allow to marinate at room temperature for 1 hour while preparing coals. Have chilled the Fresh Basil Aïoli.

Prepare coals to medium-hot, about 45 minutes. Place grill 4"–6" (10 cm–15 cm) above coals. Oil grill. Place lamb on grill, outer side down, and grill 12 minutes to sear, brushing with marinade. Turn lamb and sear other side 10 minutes. Continue to grill lamb, turning and basting, for about 35–45 minutes *total* cooking time for medium-rare, 15 minutes more for medium. Test thickest part for medium-rare with the tip of a sharp knife. Season with salt and pepper during final grilling.

While lamb is grilling, place the vegetables on the outer edges of the grill, basting with olive oil and turning until vegetables are golden brown and just crisp-tender. Remove vegetables to a platter as they are cooked.

Remove lamb from grill and allow to rest 10 minutes before carving. Carve lamb in slices, thick or thin, and place on herb-lined platter. Surround with the grilled vegetables, and serve with a generous crock of chilled Fresh Basil Aïoli for both the lamb and vegetables.

Suggested Vegetables for Grilling:

8 whole	carrots, scrubbed, with 2" (5 cm) stems intact
4	zucchini, split in half lengthwise
4	crookneck squash, split in half lengthwise
8	Japanese eggplants, left whole, stems intact
2 large	red bell peppers, quartered
2 large	green bell peppers, quartered
	olive oil
	salt and pepper

Place vegetables on oiled grill. Brush with olive oil, and grill until golden brown, with handsome grillmarks, and just tender. Season with salt and pepper during final minutes of grilling.

ARMENIAN SHISH KEBAB

This is the lamb shish kebab I am most familiar with—the one I watched my father prepare from the time I was a little girl. It was always our Sunday afternoon feast—shared around a table with close friends. Skewer the vegetables separately so that they will cook properly. Serve with a hot rice pilaf, stuffed grape-vine leaves, a fresh salad of tomatoes and onions with parsley, olive oil and lemon juice, and warm pita bread. **Serves 6.**

3 pounds (1500 grams)	boneless leg of lamb, cut into 1 1/2" (3.5 cm) cubes
2/3 cup (150 mL)	dry red wine
3 tbsp. (45 mL)	olive oil
1 large	onion, peeled and diced
3 tbsp. (45 mL)	minced fresh parsley
12	Italian plum tomatoes
3	green bell peppers, quartered
3	red onions, peeled and quartered
	salt and pepper
	sprigs of fresh parsley

In a large crockery bowl, combine the cubed lamb, red wine, olive oil, diced onion and minced parsley. Turn to coat with your hands or a spoon. Cover and marinate 2 hours at room temperature or 6 hours refrigerated. Bring lamb and marinade to room temperature before barbecuing.

Prepare coals to ashen white, about 1 hour. Place grill 4" (10 cm) above hot coals. Spread coals out in an even layer.

While coals are heating, skewer kebabs. Thread lamb on long metal skewers. Thread tomatoes, quartered peppers, and quartered onions each on separate skewers. Brush all with marinade.

Oil grill. Place skewers over hot coals, with tomatoes at nearest edge of grill. Grill lamb about 12–15 minutes total for medium-rare, onions and peppers about 15–18 minutes, and tomatoes about 5–8 minutes. Brush with any remaining marinade while grilling and turning skewers, and season with salt and pepper during final minutes of grilling.

Remove skewers from grill. Allow to rest 5 minutes. Gently push lamb off skewers, and mound on a large rustic platter. Surround with the grilled vegetables, garnish with fresh sprigs of parsley and serve at once.

MIDDLE-EASTERN LAMB BURGERS

Thick, juicy burgers made from lamb are a real treat. Flavor the ground meat with lemon, mint, onion, garlic and scallions. Serve on toasted, sesame-topped buns with sliced tomato and purple onions, or tuck inside warm pita breads with a drizzle of garlic-yogurt, shredded lettuce, and chopped tomatoes and onions. **Serves 6.**

2 pounds (1 kg)	lean ground lamb
2 cloves	garlic, peeled and pressed
2 tbsp. (30 mL)	finely grated lemon rind (yellow part only)
2 tbsp. (30 mL)	lemon juice
1	egg, beaten
1/3 cup (75 mL)	onion, finely minced
1/3 cup (75 mL)	scallions, finely minced
1/2 cup (125 mL)	finely minced, fresh mint leaves
2 tsp. (10 mL)	salt
1 tsp. (5 mL)	freshly ground black pepper
1 tsp. (5 mL)	ground cumin (optional)
2 tsp. (30 mL)	fine dry bread crumbs

Combine the ground lamb with remaining ingredients in a large bowl, using a fork or an electric mixer with a dough-hook. Handle gently. Using moistened hands, form mixture into 6 patties, each about 1" (2 cm) thick. Place on flat plate, cover loosely with waxed paper, and refrigerate 3–4 hours to blend flavors before grilling.

Prepare coals to medium-hot, about 45 minutes. Place grill 4" (10 cm) above coals. Oil grill. Bring patties to room temperature 20 minutes before grilling.

Place lamb patties on grill and sear 4–5 minutes on one side. Turn and continue to grill additional 3–4 minutes, until patties are golden brown and crusty on the outside and pink and juicy on the inside. Remove patties from grill and serve as suggested.

GREEK LAMB SHISH KEBABS

Being of Armenian heritage, shish kebabs are close to my heart. This version is Greek-inspired—redolent of good olive oil, oregano, lemon and mint. Serve with a rice pilaf, accompanying grilled vegetables, a bowl of cooling yogurt-dressed cucumbers and a crisp green salad. Add a crusty loaf of sesame-topped bread and you have a feast. **Serves 6.**

3 pounds (1500 grams)	boneless leg of lamb, cut into 1 1/2" (4 cm) cubes
1/2 cup (125 mL)	Greek olive oil
1/4 cup (50 mL)	fresh lemon juice
2 tbsp. (30 mL)	grated lemon rind
1 large	red onion, peeled and minced
3 tbsp. (45 mL)	fresh oregano leaves *or* 1 tbsp. (15 mL) dried
3 tbsp. (45 mL)	fresh mint leaves, minced *or* 1 tbsp. (15 mL) dried
3 large cloves	garlic, peeled and slivered
2 tsp. (10 mL)	cracked black peppercorns
1/3 cup (75 mL)	dry red wine
1 *each* large	green and red bell peppers, stemmed, seeded and cut into 1" (2 cm) squares
1 large	red onion, peeled and cut into 1" (2 cm) pieces
24	cherry tomatoes
	salt and pepper
	sprigs of fresh mint, as garnish

Combine the olive oil, lemon juice, rind, minced onion, oregano, mint, garlic, pepper and red wine. Whisk until completely blended. Pour marinade over lamb cubes, toss to coat, and cover and refrigerate at least 6 hours, or overnight. Turn lamb cubes several times.

Prepare coals to medium-hot, about 45 minutes. Place grill 4" (10 cm) above coals. Bring lamb to room temperature while coals are heating. Lift lamb from marinade, and thread on long metal skewers, alternating with the onion pieces and green and red peppers. Thread cherry tomatoes on a separate long skewer (as they will cook quickly).

Oil grill. Place skewers of lamb and vegetables on grill, and brush with marinade. Sear, turn skewers and brush with marinade. Sear and continue to grill until lamb is crusty and slightly charred on the outside, but a tender, rosy pink inside, about 10–15 minutes. Brush tomatoes with marinade and grill about 2–4 minutes, turning once. Season both with salt and pepper.

Remove kebabs from grill and allow to rest 5 minutes before serving. Remove meat, vegetables and cherry tomatoes gently from skewers and serve at once. Garnish with sprigs of fresh mint.

MIDDLE-EASTERN KOFTA KEBABS

In my childhood I attended many an Armenian barbecue featuring these wonderful kofta (ground meat) kebabs. The secret is in the kneading of the ground lamb with the flavorings; the result is a creamy smooth, densely packed, tender "sausage-shaped" kebab. They are wonderful tucked inside warm pita breads with chopped fresh vegetables and a tahini or yogurt dressing. And they are wonderful served as is, accompanied by a cooling tabooli cracked-wheat salad. Serves 6–8.

3 pounds (1500 grams)	lean lamb, ground twice
2 medium-large	onions, peeled and cut into chunks
3 cloves	fresh garlic, peeled and quartered
1/3 cup (75 mL)	minced fresh parsley
3 tbsp. (45 mL)	snipped fresh mint leaves, packed
3	eggs, lightly beaten
2 tsp. (10 mL)	salt
1 tsp. (5 mL)	black pepper
1 tsp. (5 mL)	*each* ground cinnamon and ground allspice
	very fine dry bread crumbs

In a food processor, chop the onions, garlic, parsley and mint to a very fine, smooth paste, scraping down sides with a rubber scraper. Add mixture to the ground lamb in a very large, deep crockery bowl. Knead mixture, with moistened hands, adding beaten eggs, salt, pepper, cinnamon and allspice. Knead mixture until very creamy and well-mixed. Cover and chill mixture 4–6 hours, or overnight.

Shape meat mixture into ovals the size of apricots. Lightly roll kebabs in fine dry bread crumbs, brushing off excess. Thread close together on long metal skewers.

Prepare coals to medium-hot, about 45 minutes. Scatter coals into an even layer. Place grill 3"–4" (7 cm–10 cm) over coals. Oil grill. Place skewers over coals, and grill kebabs, turning, about 12 minutes total for medium-rare. Kebabs should be a rich golden brown on the outside. Do not overcook, or kebabs will not be juicy.

Remove kebabs from grill, slide off skewers and serve at once.

Opposite: Grilled Racks of Lamb Provençal, assorted Grilled Vegetables (Japanese eggplant, bell peppers, zucchini, onions).

ROSY LAMB KEBABS
WITH MINTED YOGURT SAUCE

There is nothing quite as savory as rosy pink lamb done over hot coals—the
fragrant heat seals in the natural juices of the flavorful meat. Serve kebabs with
this cool, refreshing yogurt sauce, a basket of buttered and toasted pita bread,
cracked-wheat pilaf and grilled fresh eggplant and peppers. **Serves 4.**

2 1/2 pounds (1250 grams)	boneless leg of lamb, cut into 2" (5 cm) cubes
1 cup (250 mL)	dry red *or* white wine
1/3 cup (75 mL)	olive oil
2 large cloves	garlic, peeled and crushed
1 tbsp. (15 mL)	dried oregano leaves, crumbled
1 tbsp. (15 mL)	dried rosemary, crumbled
1/2	red onion, peeled and minced
	coarsely cracked black peppercorns
1 recipe	Minted Yogurt Sauce (recipe follows)
	fresh grape leaves (optional garnish)

Whisk together the wine, olive oil, garlic, oregano, rosemary, minced
onion and pepper. Place lamb cubes and marinade in a large glass or
crockery bowl, toss to coat, cover and marinate 2 hours at room
temperature.

Prepare yogurt sauce and chill several hours to blend flavors.

Prepare coals to medium-hot, about 1 hour. Lightly oil grill and place 4"
(5 cm) from source of heat. Remove lamb cubes from marinade and
thread on 4 skewers. Grill skewers over hot coals, basting frequently with
marinade, to medium-rare—about 15 minutes total. Test meat by pressing; meat should *just* yield, and not feel firm or too soft. Remove skewers
from grill and place (if desired) on a grape-leaf-lined basket or platter.
Serve kebabs sizzling hot, accompanied by the cool yogurt sauce. Salt and
pepper to taste.

Minted Yogurt Sauce

2 cups (500 mL)	plain yogurt
1 large clove	garlic, peeled and pressed
3 tbsp. (45 mL)	fresh mint leaves, finely minced
1/2 tsp. (2 mL)	salt

Whisk yogurt until smooth. Stir in garlic, minced mint and salt. Cover
and chill several hours or overnight before serving. Serve chilled or cool.

LAMB-KIDNEY BREAKFAST KEBABS

Barbecued lamb kidneys wrapped in bacon make a sensational breakfast dish on a lazy Sunday morning. Toast thick slices of sourdough bread on the grill, butter lavishly with any one of the savory butters and serve the grilled kidneys atop the toast. Accompany with grilled tomatoes, creamy scrambled eggs, cut fresh fruit and hot coffee. Serves 4–6.

8–10	fresh lamb kidneys
1/3 cup (75 mL)	olive oil
1 tbsp. (15 mL)	fresh lemon juice
1 tsp. (5 mL)	finely grated lemon rind
1 tsp. (5 mL)	dried thyme leaves
1 tsp. (5 mL)	dried rosemary, crumbled
	freshly ground coarse black pepper
8-10 slices	thick-cut bacon, blanched 1 minute, drained
	fresh sprigs thyme and rosemary
	lemon wedges
4–6 thick slices	sourdough bread, 1" (2 cm) thick, cut from a large, round loaf
1 recipe	any savory butter

Wash the kidneys under cool water. Cut in half, lengthwise. Remove any sinew or fat. Cut blanched bacon in half. Wrap outside of each kidney in bacon, and thread lengthwise on skewers. Place filled skewers in a flat, shallow dish.

Whisk together the olive oil, lemon juice, rind, thyme, rosemary and pepper. Brush over kidneys on both sides, and allow to stand 30 minutes at room temperature.

Heat coals to medium-hot, about 45 minutes. Place grill 4" (5 cm) above coals. Oil grill. Place skewers on grill and sear 4–5 minutes until golden brown. Brush with marinade in dish, and turn. Sear several minutes, until golden brown and bacon is crisped. Do not overcook; inside of kidneys should be juicy and pink (test by slashing one kidney with tip of a sharp knife). Salt to taste.

While kidneys are grilling, toast bread on outer edges of grill 1–2 minutes per side, until golden grill marks appear. Remove from grill, generously slather each piece with savory butter and place each slice on warmed plates.

Remove grilled kebabs and place directly on buttered toast. Allow to rest 5 minutes before serving. Serve hot, accompanied by sprigs of herbs and lemon wedges.

GRILLED T-BONE VEAL CHOPS WITH GREEN CHILI BUTTER AND GRILLED PEPPERS

Thick veal "T-Bones" are a real treat, especially done over charcoal with nicely charred edges. Serve with a thick slice of chilled Green Chili Butter, and accompany with grilled green bell peppers. **Serves 4.**

4	veal T-Bone chops, 1 1/4" (3 cm) thick
	olive oil
	salt and coarsely ground black pepper
4 large	green bell peppers, rinsed and halved
1 recipe	Green Chili Butter (page 27)

Prepare coals to medium-hot, about 45 minutes. Place grill 4" (10 cm) above coals. Bring veal chops to room temperature, about 20 minutes, and brush with olive oil on both sides.

Oil grill and place chops on grill. Brush peppers with olive oil and place around edge of grill, skin side down. Sear chops 3–5 minutes per side to medium-rare, seasoning with salt and pepper, and turning once. Grill peppers until tender and slightly charred, turning once.

Remove chops and peppers from grill and place on a warmed platter. Top each chop with a generous dollop of chilled Green Chili Butter while chops are sizzling hot. Serve.

GRILLED CALVES LIVER
STEAK "PERSILLADE"

We once dined on calves-liver steak in Nice, France. It still remains (some 15 years later) in our culinary memory—thick, rosy-pink, napped with a wonderful persillade sauce of fresh parsley and garlic. My version has grilled calves livers done over hot coals, with the simple sauce prepared in a heavy skillet right on the grill. Serve with potatoes roasted with olive oil and rosemary, fresh chard or spinach, crusty baguettes and a chilled Provençal Rosé.
Serves 4.

4 thick	calves-liver steaks, cut 1 1/2" (4 cm) thick; each about 8 ounces (250 grams)
4 tbsp. (60 mL)	butter, melted
2 tbsp. (30 mL)	olive oil
	salt
	coarsely ground black pepper
1 recipe	Persillade Sauce (recipe follows)

Heat coals to medium-hot, about 45 minutes. Place grill 3"–4" (7 cm–10 cm) above coals. Combine the melted butter and olive oil, and brush over liver steaks. Oil grill and place liver and grill. Sear 4 minutes on first side, brushing with butter-oil. Turn with tongs and sear other side about 4 minutes, brushing with butter-oil. Season with salt and pepper during last minute of cooking time. Total cooking time will be about 8 minutes for medium-rare. Finished liver steaks should be crusty on the outside, feel just barely firmed when pressed and be rosy-pink on the inside (test one steak by cutting in with the tip of a sharp knife).

Remove liver steaks and place on warmed plates. Immediately top each steak with several spoonfuls of the Persillade Sauce. Serve at once, piping hot.

Persillade Sauce

8 tbsp. (125 grams)	butter
4 tbsp. (60 mL)	olive oil
1/3 cup (75 mL)	shallots, finely minced
8 large cloves	garlic, peeled and finely minced (do not use a garlic press for this recipe)
1/2 cup (125 mL)	flat-leaf parsley, very finely minced (do not use a food processor; parsley must be minced by hand)
	salt
	freshly ground black pepper

In a wide, heavy, cast-iron skillet heat the butter and olive oil over medium-high heat until mixture foams. (This sauce may be prepared right on the grill while liver is cooking. Place skillet near edge of grill, over medium hot heat.) Add the shallots and sauté until softened and pale golden. Stir in the minced garlic and sauté 2 minutes. Quickly stir in the parsley and heat through until sauce bubbles. Season with salt and pepper to taste, and serve at once.

BARBECUED BREAST OF VEAL WITH PESTO

A thick, boneless breast of veal is a wonderful cut for grilling—and often ignored unless stuffed and roasted. Select a whole boneless breast without the traditional pocket for stuffing. Marinate and grill flat, then serve in thick, diagonal slices, accompanied with a heady Fresh Basil Pesto Sauce. **Serves 6.**

1 3-pound (1500-gram)	boneless veal breast
1 large	lemon, halved
2 tbsp. (30 mL)	dried basil leaves
3 large cloves	garlic, peeled and halved
1 tbsp. (15 mL)	salt
1/3 cup (75 mL)	olive oil
	freshly ground black pepper
1 recipe	Fresh Basil Pesto Sauce (see page 41)

Score the thicker-skin side of the veal breast in shallow diagonal cuts, 2" (5 cm) apart. Rub both sides of the meat with lemon juice. Sprinkle each side with 1 tbsp. (15 mL) basil. With the flat side of a chef's knife, smash the garlic into the salt and work to a paste (the salt will automatically dissolve the garlic into a paste). Rub mixture into meat on both sides. Finally, brush with olive oil and sprinkle with black pepper. Allow breast to marinate at room temperature for 1 hour while preparing coals.

Have the prepared Fresh Basil Pesto chilled and bring it to cool room temperature 10 minutes before serving.

Prepare the coals to medium-hot, about 45 minutes. Place grill 4"–6" (10 cm–15 cm) over coals. Oil grill, and place veal breast, skin side down, on grill. Sear 10 minutes, brush with any remaining marinade and turn. Sear additional side 10 minutes. Continue to cook, turning and basting, until meat is crusty and brown on the outside and tender-pink inside. Total cooking time will be about 25–30 minutes. When pressed, meat should just feel firmed, not soft.

Remove veal from grill, and place on carving board. Allow meat to rest 15 minutes before carving. Carve veal on the diagonal in 1/2" (1 cm) thick slices, serving several slices per portion. Accompany each serving with a generous dollop of pesto sauce.

FISH AND SEAFOOD ON THE GRILL

Fresh halibut steaks, in season, grilled and served with a basil-flecked tomato sauce; fresh salmon done in steaks with savory butters or flavored hollandaise sauces, hot off the grill; shrimp in citrus-laden Florida Sunshine Sauce or in a buttery and peppery Cajun Sauce; grilled soft-shelled crabs in a sizzling garlic butter; king crab legs from Alaska done over charcoal and served with a Creole Sauce for dipping; seafood brochettes; grilled clams; and a barbecued oyster roast (inspired by the first I ever encountered, at Yellow Point Lodge on Vancouver Island, right on the beach at sunset)—all take their place in the roster of good grilled fish and seafood. Fish and seafood have taken on a new dimension of pure, delicious, enthusiastic enjoyment, as the barbecue has a wonderful way with fish—sealing in the natural, sweet flavor and juices and adding the aroma of hickory, alder or other aromatic wood and chips. So whether you catch it yourself, are gifted by a friend's bounty or visit your local fishmonger—do your next batch of fish or seafood on the barbecue.

GRILLED HALIBUT STEAKS WITH FRESH BASIL-TOMATO SAUCE

Thick steaks of naturally sweet, fresh halibut are delightful done on the grill. The intense heat seals in the natural juices, and the slight charring lends a most appealing flavor. Napping each steak with a tomato sauce flavored with fresh basil adds a final fillip. **Serves 4.**

4	fresh halibut steaks, each 8–10 ounces (250–300 grams)
2 tbsp. (30 mL)	olive oil
4 tbsp. (60 mL)	butter, melted
2 tsp. (10 mL)	dried basil leaves, crumbled
	salt
	freshly ground black pepper
1 recipe	Fresh Basil-Tomato Sauce (recipe follows)
	lemon wedges
	crisp sprigs fresh basil

Prepare the tomato sauce 3–4 hours before serving and set aside until ready to use.

Combine the olive oil, melted butter and basil leaves. Brush mixture over both sides of halibut, and let sit at room temperature 20 minutes before grilling. Prepare coals to medium-hot, about 45 minutes. Lightly oil grill.

Place halibut steaks on the grill, and sear 4–5 minutes, seasoning with salt and pepper during final minute. Brush with any remaining butter-oil and turn. Sear additional 3–4 minutes, or just until fish turns opaque and begins to flake with a fork. Season with salt and pepper. Remove steaks from the grill at once and place on warmed plates. Nap each steak with several spoonfuls of barely warm Fresh Basil-Tomato Sauce. Garnish each serving with a lemon wedge and a sprig of fresh basil.

Fresh Basil-Tomato Sauce

3 tbsp. (45 mL)	olive oil
3 tbsp. (45 mL)	butter
2 large cloves	fresh garlic, peeled and minced
1 medium	onion, peeled and finely diced
3 cups (750 mL)	chopped, peeled and seeded fresh tomatoes (Italian plum tomatoes are best for this recipe)
1 tsp. (5 mL)	sugar
1 tsp. (5 mL)	fresh lemon rind, finely grated (yellow part only)
1 tbsp. (15 mL)	fresh lemon juice
1/2 tsp. (2 mL)	salt
1/4 tsp. (1 mL)	freshly ground black pepper
1/3 cup (75 mL)	snipped fresh basil

Heat the olive oil and butter in a deep, stainless steel saucepan over medium-high heat until butter foams. Add the garlic and sauté 1 minute. Stir in the onions and sauté, stirring, until softened and pale golden in color. Add the tomatoes, increase heat to high and cook 5–6 minutes until tomatoes release their juices and then re-absorb them. Stir in the sugar, lemon rind, lemon juice, salt and pepper and bring mixture to a simmer over low heat. Cook sauce, stirring occasionally, uncovered 15–18 minutes until glossy and somewhat thickened and pulpy. Stir in the snipped basil, heat 3 minutes and remove sauce from heat. Taste and correct for seasonings. Set sauce aside several hours to blend flavors.

Reheat sauce gently before serving.

CURRY-GLAZED GRILLED HALIBUT WITH CHUTNEY-GRILLED PEACHES AND PINEAPPLE

Thick fresh halibut steaks are especially good when glazed with a curry-spiked butter on the grill, accompanied by glazed grilled fresh peaches and pineapple. Serve with warm chapatis, a cool yogurt, cucumber and mint raita, and saffron rice. Ice-cold beer is the perfect accompaniment. **Serves 6.**

6 8-ounce (250-gram)	fresh halibut steaks, 1" thick (2.5 cm)
10 tbsp. (150 grams)	unsalted butter
2 tbsp. (30 mL)	vegetable oil
2 tbsp. (30 mL)	curry powder
2 tbsp. (30 mL)	fresh lemon juice
	salt
	freshly ground black pepper
	Chutney-Grilled Peaches and Pineapple (recipe follows)

Prepare coals to medium-hot, about 45 minutes to 1 hour. Melt butter in a small, heavy saucepan with the oil until butter foams. Stir in the curry powder, whisking until smooth. Stir in the lemon juice and heat until bubbly, 1 minute. Remove from heat and cool to warm.

Oil grill and place 4" (10 cm) above coals. Brush halibut steaks on one side with curry butter and place, buttered side down, on grill. Grill fish 4–5 minutes to sear, seasoning with salt and pepper during final minute. Brush uncooked side with curry butter, and turn. Sear additional 2–3 minutes, seasoning with salt and pepper. Cook until fish just turns opaque and flakes easily with a fork. Remove fish and serve at once with grilled fruit.

Chutney-Grilled Peaches and Pineapple

4 large	fresh, firm peaches, cut in half and pitted
8 slices	fresh pineapple rings or wedges
4 tbsp. (60 mL)	butter
2/3 cup (150 mL)	chutney, puréed (only if large chunks appear)
2 tbsp. (30 mL)	fresh lemon juice
1/2 tsp. (2 mL)	ground ginger
1 tbsp. (15 mL)	Whiskey or Sherry

Heat together the butter, chutney, lemon juice, ginger and Whiskey in a small saucepan and simmer for 1 minute. Remove from heat. Place fruit on oiled grill, 4" (10 cm) from coals, and brush with chutney glaze. Grill 2–3 minutes until lightly glazed and charred, brush with glaze and turn. Grill remaining side, brushing with glaze, 2–3 minutes. Remove fruit and serve with halibut. Drizzle with any remaining chutney glaze.

GRILLED SWORDFISH STEAKS
WITH ANCHOVY-BUTTER SAUCE

Nothing is better than thick, meaty swordfish steaks done on the grill. And a perfect complement is this pungent, anchovy-spiked butter sauce, with lemon and garlic. The sauce may be prepared ahead of time and served at room temperature. Serve this dish with tiny, roasted red potatoes, and braised fresh spinach with toasted pine nuts. A crusty loaf of French bread is ideal for soaking up the rich sauce. **Serves 4.**

4 large	fresh swordfish steaks, cut 1" (2.5 cm) thick; 10–12 ounces (300–375 grams) each
	olive oil
	salt
	freshly ground black pepper
	Anchovy Butter Sauce (recipe follows)
	sprigs of Italian flat-leaf parsley

Brush both sides of swordfish with olive oil. Season with salt and freshly ground black pepper. Allow to sit 20 minutes before grilling.

Lightly oil grill and place fish over hot coals 4" (10 cm) from source of heat. Grill 5–6 minutes on each side or until steaks turn white and are *just* firmed and are slightly charred on either side. Do not overcook. Serve grilled fish with prepared Anchovy Butter Sauce. Garnish with sprigs of parsley and serve sizzling hot.

Anchovy Butter Sauce

10	anchovy filets
2	egg yolks, at room temperature
2 cloves	fresh garlic, peeled and pressed
4 tbsp. (60 mL)	minced fresh parsley
1 tbsp. (15 mL)	Dijon mustard
2 tbsp. (30 mL)	fresh lemon juice
2 tsp. (10 mL)	finely grated lemon rind
1/4 pound (125 grams)	very fresh butter, melted and hot
1/2 cup (125 mL)	olive oil
	coarse grindings black peppercorns

In a food processor, purée the anchovy filets, egg yolks and garlic to a paste. Add parsley and continue to process to a paste. Add mustard, lemon juice and rind. Combine the hot melted butter and olive oil in a measuring cup with a spout. With the motor running, begin pouring the butter-oil in a *very* thin, slow, steady stream. Continue until mixture is emulsified and thickened. Finished sauce should be like a grainy mayonnaise. Season with black pepper. Serve at room temperature or chilled as a topping for hot, grilled fish.

GRILLED SWORDFISH STEAKS WITH ROSEMARY-ORANGE-CURRANT BUTTER

Add savory butter to sizzling swordfish steaks as they come off the coals—the wonderful complementary flavors of rosemary, orange and currants are a delight with the swordfish. **Serves 4.**

4 large	swordfish steaks, cut 3/4" (2 cm) thick; 8–10 ounces (250–300 grams) each
	olive oil
	salt
	freshly ground black pepper
1 recipe	Rosemary-Orange-Currant Butter (page 22)

Brush both sides of swordfish with olive oil. Season with salt and freshly ground black pepper. Lightly oil grill, and place fish over hot coals 4" (10 cm) from heat. Grill 5–6 minutes on one side, turn and grill 2–3 minutes on remaining side *just* until fish turns white and is just firmed. Do not overcook.

Top each sizzling swordfish steak with a large slice of prepared, chilled flavored butter. Serve at once.

BARBECUED RED SNAPPER VERACRUZ

Anyone who has traveled to Mexico has come back with a fondness for any kind of fish done "veracruz-style"—a wonderful fresh tomato sauce with onion, green olives, and capers. Fresh red snapper filets are traditional, and delicious in this recipe. Serve with a fresh avocado and orange salad, black beans, rice and warm corn tortillas. **Serves 4.**

4 10-ounce (300-gram)	fresh red snapper filets
	olive oil
	fresh limes
	salt and pepper
1 recipe	Salsa Veracruz (recipe follows)
	additional green olives stuffed with pimiento
	crisp sprigs fresh cilantro (fresh coriander or Chinese parsley)
	lime wedges

Prepare Salsa Veracruz several hours before serving (or the night before), and reheat very gently before serving.

Prepare coals to medium-hot, about 45 minutes. Brush snapper filets with olive oil and lime juice, and allow to sit 20 minutes. Lightly oil grill. Place snapper filets on grill, 4" (10 cm) from source of heat, and sear 4–5 minutes. Season with salt and pepper. Brush with additional lime-oil and turn filets. Sear on remaining side an additional 2–3 minutes or just until fish turns opaque and flakes with a fork. Do not overcook.

Remove grilled snapper to warmed plates. Nap each portion with a generous spoonful of warm Salsa Veracruz. Scatter with additional whole green olives, crisp sprigs of cilantro and lime wedges. Serve at once.

Salsa Veracruz

(Serves 4)

1/3 cup (75 mL)	Spanish olive oil
1 large	onion, peeled and thinly sliced
2 cloves	garlic, peeled and slivered
1	green bell pepper, thinly sliced
3 cups (750 mL)	fresh tomatoes, coarsely chopped
1 tbsp. (15 mL)	sugar
1 tbsp. (15 mL)	Spanish paprika
1 tbsp. (15 mL)	Sherry vinegar *or* red wine vinegar
1/4 cup (60 mL)	dry Sherry wine
3 tbsp. (45 mL)	capers, drained
1/2 cup (125 mL)	pimiento-stuffed large green onions, thinly sliced
1/2 tsp. (2 mL)	salt
	freshly ground black pepper, to taste
6–8 drops	liquid hot pepper (Tabasco)
3 tbsp. (45 mL)	minced fresh parsley
	additional olives, as garnish

Heat the olive oil over medium-high heat in a large skillet. Add the onions, garlic and green pepper. Sauté, stirring, until vegetables are softened and pale golden brown. Add the chopped tomatoes. Increase heat to high, and sauté until tomatoes release their juices and then reabsorb them—about 5–7 minutes. Stir in the sugar, paprika, vinegar and Sherry. Cook, stirring, 3–4 minutes until bubbly and thickened. Reduce heat to medium, and add the capers and olives. Season with the salt, pepper and Tabasco. Heat sauce through, stirring occasionally, 5–6 minutes. Finally, stir in the minced parsley and remove sauce from heat. Let cool 10 minutes.

Serve sauce warm over grilled red snapper. Garnish with additional olives, if desired.

GRILLED SWORDFISH
AND JAPANESE EGGPLANT
WITH PARMESAN-GARLIC BUTTER

This combination of flavors is unbeatable! Thick swordfish steks and slender Japanese eggplants are grilled and topped with generous chunks of Parmesan-butter. Accompany with spaghettini coated with fresh basil pesto, a crisp romaine salad and hot garlic bread. **Serves 4.**

4	fresh swordfish steaks, 1 1/2" (4 cm) thick; about 10 ounces (300 grams) each
8	Japanese eggplants
	olive oil
	fresh lemons, cut into wedges
	salt and freshly ground black pepper
1 recipe	Parmesan-Garlic Butter (page 28)

Prepare coals to medium-hot, about 45 minutes. Oil grill. Brush swordfish with olive oil and place on center of grill. Brush whole eggplants with olive oil and place around outer perimeter of grill. Cook 4–5 minutes, season with salt and pepper and turn swordfish and eggplants. Brush with additional olive oil and cook another 4–5 minutes—just until eggplants are softened and tender, and swordfish is opaque and just begins to flake with a fork.

Remove swordfish and eggplants to a large warmed platter. Top with chilled slices of Parmesan-Garlic Butter. Garnish with lemon wedges and serve at once.

Opposite: Cajun Peppered Shrimp Feast.

GRILLED CATFISH FILETS
WITH NEW ORLEANS CREOLE SAUCE

*Catfish filets hold up beautifully to the heat of a charcoal grill. The hot filets, infused with the fragrance of bay leaves, are napped with generous spoonfuls of this hearty Creole sauce, straight from the heart of New Orleans. Serve with a skillet of hot cornbread and a crisp green salad with vinaigrette and toasted pecans. **Serves 4.***

4 8-ounce (250-gram)	fresh catfish filets
2 tbsp. (30 mL)	melted butter
3 tbsp. (45 mL)	peanut oil
1 tsp. (5 mL)	paprika
1/4 tsp. (1 mL)	cayenne pepper
1/4 tsp. (1 mL)	ground allspice
1/2 tsp. (2 mL)	thyme leaves
1 recipe	New Orleans Creole Sauce (page 39)
16	bay leaves, soaked 30 minutes in warm water, drained
	crisp bunches of fresh bay leaves (optional garnish)

Soak the bay leaves as directed, then drain. Prepare the New Orleans Creole Sauce up to three days in advance, and reheat gently before serving.

Combine the melted butter, peanut oil, paprika, cayenne, allspice and thyme leaves and heat together in a small saucepan 2 minutes. Set aside 15 minutes to cool slightly. Brush over both sides of catfish filets and allow to stand 20 minutes before grilling.

Lightly oil grill with peanut oil. Place drained bay leaves directly on hot coals. Place fish filets on grill 4" (10 cm) from coals. Grill fish 4 minutes on one side, turn and grill 3–4 minutes on other side. Cook only until fish turns opaque, is slightly charred and *just* feels slightly firmed when pressed. Season with salt and pepper.

Serve piping hot catfish filets on warmed plates, napped with generous spoonfuls of warm New Orleans Creole Sauce. Garnish, if desired, with bay-leaf clusters.

GRILLED TROUT MEUNIÈRE

The classic trout meunière is even more delicious done on the grill. Serve with a rice pilaf and fresh green beans with toasted almonds for a sensational supper. Serves 4.

4 12-ounce (375-gram)	fresh whole trout, gutted
12 thin slices	fresh lemon
4 large	bay leaves
	salt
	freshly ground black pepper
2 tbsp. (30 mL)	butter
2 tbsp. (30 mL)	olive oil
1 recipe	Meunière Sauce (recipe follows)
3 tbsp. (45 mL)	minced fresh parsley
2 tbsp. (30 mL)	minced fresh chives
	notched lemon slices, as garnish

Season the cavities of each trout with salt and pepper, and stuff each with 3 slices lemon and 1 bay leaf. Press trout closed and place in an oiled, double-hinged fish basket. Grill trout over hot coals, 4"–6" (10 cm–15 cm) from source of heat, until lightly charred and fish just begins to flake, 3–4 minutes per side.

While trout is grilling, prepare the Meunière Sauce. Remove trout from the grill. Place each on a warmed plate and spoon a generous 2 tbsp. (30 mL) butter sauce over each trout. Sprinkle with minced parsley and chives, garnish with lemon slices and serve very hot.

Meunière Sauce

1 cup (250 grams)	very fresh butter
3 tbsp. (45 mL)	fresh lemon juice
1/4 tsp. (1 mL)	freshly ground black pepper

Melt the butter in a small, heavy skillet or saucepan over low heat until butter turns a rich, deep golden brown (do not allow butter to burn). Stir in the lemon juice and pepper, and heat sauce 1 minute until bubbly. Serve at once.

GRILLED TROUT AMANDINE GALATOIRE'S-STYLE

My favorite dish in all of New Orleans is one of the simplest—the superb Trout Meunière Amandine at Galatoire's. This dish alone warrants a visit to this Fresh Quarter landmark. My own version teams the Amandine Meunière Sauce with charcoal-grilled trout, and the contrast is delicious. Serve New Orleans style—with crunchy, deep-fried eggplant sticks, brown oven-roasted potatoes and a Bibb-lettuce salad. Serves 4.

4 10-ounce (300-gram)	thick, speckled trout filets
	salt
	freshly ground black pepper
2 tbsp. (30 mL)	butter
2 tbsp. (30 mL)	oil
1 recipe	Amandine Meunière Sauce (recipe follows)
	lemon wedges
	fresh parsley

Melt butter and oil together and brush over both sides of the trout filets. Season with salt and pepper. Place filets in an oiled, double-hinged fish basket. Grill trout over hot coals, 4"–6" (10 cm–15 cm) from source of heat, until slightly charred and fish just begins to flake, 3–4 minutes per side.

While trout is grilling, prepare the Amandine Meunière Sauce. Remove trout from grill, place filets on warmed plates and divide sauce over each serving. Serve at once, sizzling hot, garnished with parsley.

Amandine Meunière Sauce

1 cup (250 grams)	very fresh butter
1 cup (250 mL)	sliced almonds, toasted
3 tbsp. (45 mL)	fresh lemon juice

Toast almonds in a 325° F. (160° C.) oven 8–10 minutes until a rich golden brown, stirring once or twice. Melt butter in a deep, heavy saucepan, whipping constantly, until butter is frothy, bubbly and a rich golden brown. Stir in the toasted almonds and the lemon juice, heat 1 minute more until bubbly and pour at once over hot trout filets.

BARBECUED SALMON FILETS WITH HERBED MAYONNAISE

This method of grilling any kind of fresh fish is so simple and so good that it is destined to become a favorite. Select any fresh herb you wish, suiting it to the fish you are grilling. With these salmon filets, fresh dill is especially nice, but try tarragon with halibut, basil with swordfish and thyme with snapper—or use your own favorites. **Serves 4.**

4 thick	salmon filets, each 8–10 ounces (250–300 grams)
1 cup (250 mL)	best-quality mayonnaise
3 tbsp. (45 mL)	finely minced fresh herbs (dillweed for this recipe) *or* 1 1/2 tsp. (7 mL) dried herbs
1 tbsp. (15 mL)	minced fresh parsley
1 clove	fresh garlic, peeled and minced
1 tbsp. (15 mL)	fresh lemon juice
	salt and pepper
	fresh herbs, as garnish
	lemon wedges

Whisk together the mayonnaise, selected herbs, parsley, garlic and lemon juice. Chill several hours to blend flavors. Prepare coals to medium-hot, about 45 minutes. Place grill 4" (10 cm) above heat. Bring salmon filets to room temperature, 20 minutes. Oil grill.

Measure out 1/2 cup (125 mL) herbed mayonnaise. Chill remainder until serving time. Brush 1 tbsp. (15 mL) mayonnaise over each filet on skin-side. Place on grill, skin-side down, and sear 4 minutes. Brush uncooked sides with 1 tbsp. (15 mL) mayonnaise each, and turn. Sear additional 3–4 minutes, or until fish turns opaque and begins to flake easily with a fork. Season with salt and pepper, and remove from grill to warmed plates.

Top each portion with 2 tbsp. (30 mL) reserved chilled mayonnaise. Garnish with fresh herbs and lemon wedges. Serve at once.

FAR-EAST BARBECUED B.C. SALMON

Thick fresh salmon steaks bathed in this fragrant marinade and char-grilled are superb. Serve with grilled scallions, steamed brown rice, and a crisp spinach salad tossed with toasted peanuts. **Serves 4.**

4	fresh salmon steaks, 1" thick (2.5 cm)
1/3 cup (75 mL)	dry Sherry
1/3 cup (75 mL)	soy sauce
1/4 cup (50 mL)	peanut oil
2 tbsp. (30 mL)	Oriental sesame oil
2 tbsp. (30 mL)	rice wine vinegar
2 tbsp. (30 mL)	brown sugar, packed
	salt and freshly ground black pepper
8	long scallions, rinsed and patted dry

Place salmon steaks in a single layer in a glass dish. Whisk together the Sherry, soy sauce, peanut oil, sesame oil, vinegar and brown sugar. Pour marinade over salmon steaks, turning once to coat. Cover and refrigerate 2 hours.

Prepare coals to medium-hot, about 45 minutes. Place grill 4" (10 cm) above source of heat. Bring salmon to room temperature. Oil grill.

Place salmon steaks on grill, reserving marinade. Grill salmon 4–5 minutes per side, or just until salmon turns opaque and begins to flake with a fork. Place whole scallions on grill, brush with marinade, and grill 2–3 minutes until golden.

Meanwhile, while salmon is grilling, heat reserved marinade in a small saucepan until syrupy and reduced to 4 tbsp. (60 mL). Remove salmon from grill and place on warmed plates. Top each steak with 1 tbsp. (15 mL) reduced marinade and garnish with 2 scallions. Serve at once.

GRILLED B.C. SALMON STEAKS WITH SAVORY WATERCRESS-MUSTARD BUTTER

Cut thick salmon steaks, quickly grill over hot coals and serve slightly charred, with a generous portion of Savory Watercress-Mustard Butter on each salmon steak. **Serves 4.**

4 fresh	salmon steaks, cut 1" (2.5 cm) thick; each about 10 ounces (300 grams)
2 tbsp. (30 mL)	melted butter
2 tbsp. (30 mL)	oil
	salt
	freshly ground white peppercorns
1 recipe	Savory Watercress-Mustard Butter (page 25)
	fresh watercress, for garnish

Prepare the flavored butter and chill several hours or overnight.

Combine the melted butter and oil, and brush over both sides of salmon steaks. Season with salt and white pepper, and let stand 15 minutes. Lightly oil grill and set 4" (10 cm) above hot coals. Place salmon steaks on grill and cook about 4 minutes on each side or until fish *just* turns opaque, is charred a lovely brown and feels slightly firmed when pressed. Remove steaks from grill and place on warmed plates. Top each steak with a large spoonful or slice of Savory Watercress-Mustard Butter. Serve at once, garnished with watercress.

GRILLED B.C. SALMON
WITH SPICY RED PEPPER HOLLANDAISE

The combination of fresh salmon hot off the grill with a rich red-pepper-spiked hollandaise sauce is unbeatable. Serve garnished with a pretty tomato-rose, accompany with crisp tender haricot verts and tiny, steamed red potatoes.
Serves 4.

4 thick	fresh salmon filets, each about 8 ounces (250 grams)
2 tbsp. (30 mL)	unsalted butter
2 tbsp. (30 mL)	olive oil
1 recipe	Spicy Red Pepper Hollandaise (recipe follows)

Prepare the coals to medium-hot, about 1 hour. Lightly oil the grill, and set 4"–6" (10 cm–15 cm) above coals. Prepare the hollandaise sauce while heating coals and set aside.

Melt the 2 tbsp. (30 mL) *each* butter and olive oil together in a small skillet, and brush over salmon filets. Place filets on oiled grill, and cook about 3–4 minutes on each side or *just* until fish can barely be flaked with a fork. Do not overcook.

Spoon a pool of barely warm sauce on each of 4 serving plates, and set salmon filets in center of sauce. Nap each serving with additional spoonful of sauce and serve at once.

Spicy Red Pepper Hollandaise

2 large	egg yolks, at room temperature
1 tbsp. (15 mL)	fresh lemon juice
1/3 cup (75 mL)	roasted red pepper, drained and diced
2 tbsp. (30 mL)	tomato paste
1/2 tsp. (2 mL)	chili powder
	pinch sugar
1/2 pound (250 grams)	fresh unsalted butter, melted and warm
	salt

In a food processor (or blender), process the egg yolks, lemon juice, roasted red pepper, tomato paste and chili powder. Add a small pinch of sugar. With the motor running, add the hot melted butter in a very slow, steady, thin stream until sauce is completely smooth and emulsified. Season to taste with salt. Keep sauce just barely warm, not hot, for best flavor.

BARBECUED SALMON FILETS WITH GREEN PEPPERCORN-LIME BUTTER

Serve fresh grilled salmon filets glazed with this unusual green peppercorn and lime butter. Accompany with roasted new potatoes and fresh green beans for a memorable meal. **Serves 4**

4 thick	salmon filets, each about 8–10 ounces (250–300 grams)
4 tbsp. (60 mL)	butter, melted
1 tbsp. (15 mL)	nut-flavored oil (walnut or hazelnut)
1 tbsp. (15 mL)	fresh lime juice
	salt
	freshly ground black pepper
1 recipe	Green Peppercorn-Lime Butter (page 23)
	fresh lime wedges or slices

Prepare coals to medium-hot, about 45 minutes. Place grill 4" (10 cm) above source of heat. Bring salmon filets to room temperature, about 20 minutes. Combine melted butter, oil and lime juice and brush over skin-side of filets. Oil grill and place filets on grill, skin-side down. Sear filets 4 minutes, seasoning with salt and pepper during last minute. Brush filets with additional butter mixture, and turn. Grill additional 4 minutes, or just until fish turns opaque and begins to flake with a fork. Season with salt and pepper at finish.

Remove grilled filets from heat, place on warmed plates and top each with a generous chunk of chilled Green Peppercorn-Lime Butter. Garnish with lime wedges or slices and serve at once.

CAJUN PEPPERED SHRIMP FEAST

"Barbecue Shrimp," a local favorite in New Orleans, are misnamed as they aren't barbecued at all. But these are and they are terrific, messy, great fun to peel and eat, and need only pitchers of ice-cold beer to wash them down and loaves of hot, crusty French bread to soak up every last bit of the wonderful sauce. Invite fun-loving friends over, and dig in! **Serves 6–8.**

4 pounds (2 kg)	fresh jumbo shrimp (prawns) in the shell
1 pound (500 grams)	very fresh butter
1 cup (125 mL)	olive oil
10 cloves	fresh garlic, peeled and pressed
6 whole	bay leaves, crumbled
1 tsp. (5 mL)	*each* dried oregano, thyme, rosemary crumbled
1 tsp. (5 mL)	*each* salt, cayenne pepper, black pepper
1 tbsp. (15 mL)	Spanish paprika
15 drops	liquid hot-pepper sauce (Tabasco)
2 tbsp. (30 mL)	fresh lemon juice
	grated rind from 1 lemon
	lemon wedges, as garnish

In a very large, heavy, iron skillet melt the butter slowly over low heat until bubbly. Stir in all remaining ingredients, except for the lemon wedges. Whisk until smooth. Bring mixture to a simmer, and cook sauce uncovered, stirring occasionally, 15 minutes until bubbly and flavors are blended. Remove from heat and allow sauce to stand 45 minutes.

Butterfly the raw shrimp by slitting underside half-way through lengthwise, leaving shell intact. Gently pull off legs and discard. Place shrimp in a large bowl or shallow pan and add half the sauce. Toss gently to coat with sauce and let shrimp marinate 45 minutes while preparing coals. Reserve remaining sauce.

Prepare coals to medium-hot, about 45 minutes. Place grill 4" (10 cm) over source of heat. Oil grill or a double-hinged basket. Remove shrimp from sauce and place on grill or in basket. Barbecue shrimp 2–4 minutes until bright red, brushing with sauce in bowl. Turn shrimp and cook additional 2–3 minutes, brushing with sauce. Shrimp are cooked when they are bright red, just firmed and opaque. Do not overcook, or shrimp will be tough.

Gently reheat reserved sauce and serve for dipping. Serve accompanied by fresh lemon wedges, and provide a bucket or large bowl for the shells.

MESQUITE-GRILLED JUMBO PRAWNS WITH FRESH GREEN SALSA

The current rage for anything mesquite-grilled is well deserved, for a handful of soaked chips added to hot coals imparts a wonderful smoky flavor like no other. Try serving these prawns, or jumbo shrimp, with a cool black-bean salad, steamed rice and grilled red peppers. **Serves 4.**

1 1/2 pounds (750 grams)	prawns (jumbo shrimp), shelled and deveined, tails left intact
4 tbsp. (60 mL)	butter, melted
6 tbsp. (90 mL)	olive oil
2 tsp. (10 mL)	chili powder
1 tsp. (5 mL)	ground cumin
1/2 tsp. (2 mL)	paprika
1 large clove	garlic, peeled and pressed
2 tbsp. (30 mL)	fresh lemon juice
1 recipe	Fresh Green Salsa (recipe follows) fresh cilantro (Chinese parsley, fresh coriander)

Combine the melted butter, olive oil, chili powder, cumin, paprika, pressed garlic and lemon juice in a small saucepan and simmer 2–3 minutes to blend flavors. Set aside to cool 20 minutes.

Prepare salsa several hours ahead to blend flavors, and chill before serving.

Soak 8–10 mesquite chips in warm water for 30 minutes; drain. While chips are soaking, brush prawns on both sides with flavored butter marinade, and allow to sit 20 minutes at room temperature.

Lightly oil grill, and place 4" (10 cm) above white-hot coals. Place drained mesquite chips directly on coals. Grill prawns about 2 minutes on each side, or *just* until firmed and opaque. Remove from grill and serve sizzling hot, accompanied by the salsa and fresh cilantro.

Fresh Green Salsa

10	tomatillos (Mexican green tomatoes with thin, papery husks; available where Latin produce is sold)
2 cloves	garlic, peeled and pressed
1/2 cup (125 mL)	scallions (green onions) trimmed and very thinly sliced
1/4 cup (75 mL)	fresh cilantro, finely minced
2 tbsp. (30 mL)	minced fresh parsley
1	jalapeño pepper, stemmed, seeded and finely minced
2 tbsp. (30 mL)	fresh lemon juice
2 tbsp. (30 mL)	olive oil
1	Hass avocado, peeled, seeded and diced
	salt
	fresh ground black pepper

Peel off the husks from the tomatillos; wash, stem and cut into coarse dice. Bring to a simmer with the garlic in a small, heavy saucepan 3–4 minutes, or until tomatillos are just tender. Set aside to cool 30 minutes.

In a food processor, chop the cooled tomatillo mixture, scallions, cilantro, parsley, jalapeño pepper and lemon juice, using quick "on-off" turns, and scraping down sides with a rubber spatula. Add olive oil and blend 5 seconds. Finally, add the diced avocado, and give several "on-off" turns to chop. Finished salsa should be slightly smooth, slightly chunky. Season to taste with salt and pepper. Chill until ready to serve.

BARBECUED WHOLE SALMON OVER FENNEL WITH PERNOD BUTTER

All along the sun-drenched French Riviera one finds fresh fish grillé au fenouil (grilled over dried fennel twigs). This delicately perfumed treatment nicely complements a whole fresh salmon. Try a savory melt of chilled Pernod Butter to glaze the delicate fish and serve with a crisp, iced Graves or Blanc de Blanc, tiny, steamed, red potatoes in butter and fresh green asparagus.

1 whole	fresh salmon, 3–3 1/2 pounds (1–1 1/2 kg), cleaned and scaled with head and tail intact
6 tbsp. (90 mL)	butter
1/3 cup (75 mL)	finely minced fresh shallots
6 tbsp. (90 mL)	nut-flavored oil (walnut or hazelnut) juice of 1 lemon
2 tsp. (30 mL)	dried fennel seeds, crushed
2 tbsp. (30 mL)	minced fresh parsley
12 dried	fennel twigs *or* 4 tbsp. (60 mL) dried fennel seeds
1 recipe	Pernod Butter (page 29) salt and freshly ground black pepper lemon wedges

Bring the salmon to room temperature, 20 minutes. Sauté the minced shallots in the butter over low heat, stirring, until softened and pale in color. Whisk in the oil, lemon juice, crushed fennel seeds and parsley. Remove from heat and cool to room temperature. Soak the dried fennel twigs in warm water 1 hour and drain.

Prepare the coals to ashen white, about 1 hour or longer. Brush cavity of salmon with butter mixture. Place salmon in an oiled, hinged fish basket. Brush outside of salmon with butter mixture.

Push coals aside, making a trough as wide as the fish basket. Scatter fennel twigs (or seeds, if substituting) over coals. Place grill 6" (15 cm) from coals. Place basket on grill and cook fish 10–12 minutes on one side, brushing with butter mixture. Turn basket, and grill remaining side 10–12 minutes. Fish is done when opaque, firmed, and just beginning to flake with a fork at its thickest section.

Remove salmon from the grill, allow fish to rest 5 minutes and carefully remove from basket with a long spatula. Transfer salmon to a large, warmed platter.

Immediately top salmon with chilled slices of Pernod Butter, allowing butter to melt over salmon and glaze surface. Serve in thick portions, separating carefully, accompanied by additional butter if desired.

FLORIDA SUNSHINE SHRIMP

The Sunshine State, famed for its oranges, inspires this citrus-sweet sauce, chunky with ground orange and chili sauce, and sweetened with honey. Soak jumbo shrimp in the sauce for 45 minutes while preparing the hot coals, pop them on the grill, and enjoy in minutes. **Serves 4.**

2 pounds (1 kg)	jumbo shrimp (prawns), shelled and deveined, with tails left intact
1 large	seedless orange, ground (including rind)
4 tbsp. (60 mL)	fresh lemon juice
2/3 cup (150 mL)	bottled chili sauce (the variety used for shrimp cocktails and hamburgers)
1/3 cup (75 mL)	honey
2 large cloves	garlic, peeled and pressed
2 tbsp. (30 mL)	Worcestershire sauce
1 tsp. (5 mL)	chili powder
1/3 cup (75 mL)	corn oil
	salt
	freshly ground black pepper

Combine the ground orange, lemon juice, chili sauce, honey, garlic, Worcestershire sauce, chili powder and corn oil in a small stainless steel saucepan. Bring to a simmer for 5 minutes over low heat, stirring. Remove from heat and cool completely.

Place shrimp in the cooled sauce and marinate 45 minutes while preparing coals. Heat coals to medium-hot and place grill 4" (10 cm) above source of heat. Oil grill with corn oil. Remove the shrimp from marinade, shake off excess sauce and place directly on grill. Sear 1 minute, baste with marinade and turn. Grill additional 2–3 minutes, or until shrimp *just* turns opaque. Do not overcook. Remove shrimp, and serve at once, accompanied by remainder of sauce for dipping.

SZECHWAN-GRILLED SHRIMP ON WARM ORIENTAL NOODLES

Serve the hot, crispy shrimp over a bed of warm Oriental noodles tossed with scallions and additional sauce. Add crisp, stir-fried snow peas (mange tout), grilled fresh pineapple-wedges and icy cold lager for a complete meal.
Serves 4.

2 pounds (1 kg)	fresh jumbo shrimp (prawns), shelled and deveined with tails left intact
1 recipe	Spicy Szechwan Sauce (page 42)
12 ounces (375 grams)	dried Oriental noodles
2 tbsp. (30 mL)	sesame oil
2/3 cup (150 mL)	minced scallions
1/2 cup (125 mL)	coarsely chopped, salted cocktail peanuts
	whole scallions, as garnish

Prepare the Spicy Szechwan Sauce ahead of time and set aside.

Prepare coals to medium-hot, about 45 minutes. While coals are heating, cook noodles al dente, rinse and toss with the sesame oil to coat. Toss with minced scallions and 1/2 cup (125 mL) Spicy Szechwan Sauce. Place noodles on warmed oval platter, and sprinkle with chopped peanuts. Keep warm while grilling shrimp.

Oil grill. Brush shrimp generously with sauce and place on grill. Sear 1–2 minutes, brush with additional sauce and grill additional 1–2 minutes. Cook shrimp just until opaque and red in color. Do not overcook. Remove shrimp from grill and place on bed of prepared warm noodles. Garnish with scallion brushes and serve at once.

Scallion Brushes

To prepare scallion brushes, select medium-sized scallions (spring, or green, onions). Trim off root end. Cut off green section so white and green sections are equal in length. Lay scallion flat on cutting surface. Using a sharp paring knife, cut slashes up through length of white part four times. Place scallions in ice-water so that slashed end will curl back. Soak scallions in refrigerator several hours or overnight. Drain before using.

GRILLED SOFT-SHELLED CRABS WITH SIZZLING GARLIC BUTTER

If you are lucky enough to find fresh soft-shelled crabs, one of the most delectable of shellfish, then try them this way—grilled over hot coals with sizzling garlic-butter. They take minutes to cook, seconds to devour! Figure on 2–3 crabs, minimum, per person. **Serves 4.**

12 (minimum)	fresh soft-shelled crabs, cleaned and patted dry
1/2 cup (125 mL)	clarified butter (see recipe for instructions)
4 large cloves	fresh, garlic, peeled and minced
1 tsp. (5 mL)	paprika
	salt
	freshly ground black pepper

Clarify 1 pound (500 grams) unsalted butter by heating over very low heat in a small, heavy suacepan. Skim off white foam (white dairy solids which burn easily) as it rises to top surface. Pour remaining clear butter into a glass jar. Cool. Measure out 1/2 cup (125 mL) for this recipe, and chill remainder until needed at another time.

Heat clarified butter with the minced garlic until garlic is tender, 4–5 minutes, stirring over the lowest heat. Brush over prepared crabs.

Lightly oil grill, and place over hot coals 6" (15 cm) from source of heat. Place buttered crabs on grill and cook 2–3 minutes per side, or just until crabs turn pinkish red, brushing crabs with garlic butter as they grill. Remove crabs to a large warmed platter, and season to taste with salt and freshly ground black pepper. Drizzle any remaining garlic butter over hot crabs and serve at once.

ORIENTAL SCALLOP KEBABS

*Grilling fresh scallops over coals is ideal, as their natural juiciness is sealed in and the subtle charred flavor is delectable. This simple marinade, and the addition of smoky bacon, makes for savory results. Serve with steamed brown rice tossed with scallions and roasted, chopped peanuts, and a stir-fry of Chinese snow peas and carrots. **Serves 4.***

1 1/2 pounds (750 grams)	fresh scallops, each about 1 1/2" (4 cm) in diameter
8 thick slices	smoked bacon, cut into 1" (2.5 cm) pieces
1/3 cup (75 mL)	soy sauce
2 tbsp. (30 mL)	peanut oil
2 tbsp. (30 mL)	Oriental toasted sesame oil
2 tbsp. (30 mL)	rice wine vinegar *or* Sherry wine vinegar
2 tbsp. (30 mL)	light brown sugar
2 tbsp. (30 mL)	dry Sherry
1 tbsp. (15 mL)	finely grated fresh ginger
1 large clove	garlic, peeled and pressed

Partially blanch bacon 3 minutes in simmering water, drain and pat dry. Thread scallions on skewers, piercing them through *horizontally* (through their diameter), and interspersing with bacon pieces. Lay filled skewers in a glass baking dish. (If using wooden bamboo skewers, soak in warm water to cover 30 minutes before threading. This will prevent skewers from excessive burning during grilling.)

Whisk together the soy sauce, peanut oil, sesame oil, vinegar, brown sugar, Sherry, ginger and garlic. Pour marinade over kebabs, and refrigerate 1–2 hours, turning several times.

Lightly oil grill. Hot coals should be moderate in temperature. Set kebabs on grill 4" (10 cm) above coals and barbecue a total of 6–7 minutes, turning once. Scallops should be lightly charred and just opaque throughout. Brush with additional marinade during final minutes of grilling. Remove from grill and serve at once. Season with salt and pepper.

Opposite: (Top to bottom) Grilled Halibut Steaks with Fresh Basil-Tomato Sauce, Grilled B.C. Salmon with Spicy Red Pepper Hollandaise.

SEAFOOD BROCHETTES
WITH SAVORY BUTTER

Serve seafood brochettes hot off the grill with any one of the savory flavored butters in this book or with Homemade Tartare Sauce. **Serves 4.**

8 slices	smoked bacon, thick-sliced, half-cooked until translucent; cut into 1 1/2" (4 cm) pieces
1 pound (500 grams)	large shrimp, peeled, deveined, tails left intact
1 pound (500 grams)	fresh sea scallops
1 pound (500 grams)	fresh swordfish steaks, 1" (2.5 cm) thick, then cut into 1" x 1 1/2" (2.5 cm x 4 cm) cubes
16	cherry tomatoes
16	pieces fresh zucchini squash, 1 1/2" (4 cm), thick
16	mushroom caps, tightly closed, wiped with a damp cloth
8 tbsp. (125 grams)	unsalted butter, melted
4 tbsp. (60 mL)	vegetable oil
1 clove	garlic, peeled and minced
2 tbsp. (30 mL)	fresh lemon juice
2 tsp. (10 mL)	paprika
	salt and freshly ground black pepper
	selected savory butter *or* Homemade Tartare Sauce (page 42)

Select 8 short skewers or 4 long skewers. Thread shrimp, scallops and swordfish cubes on skewers, alternating with bacon pieces (next to the seafood), cherry tomatoes, zucchini and mushrooms.

Combine the melted butter, vegetable oil, garlic, lemon juice and paprika in a small saucepan and simmer 1 minute. Allow to cool to room temperature. Prepare coals to medium-hot, about 45 minutes. Place grill 4" (10 cm) above source of heat. Brush prepared skewers with melted butter mixture.

Place skewers on oiled grill and sear 3–4 minutes on each side, basting with butter mixture. Season with salt and pepper during final 2 minutes cooking time. Finished brochettes should be a golden brown, with crisped edges, and the seafood should *just* be opaque.

Remove brochettes from grill. Serve at once, accompanied by a crock of softened savory butter or chilled tartare sauce.

KING CRAB LEGS
WITH CREOLE HOLLANDAISE

What could be better than jumbo Alaskan king crab legs, split and grilled with butter to a slightly charred finish? Perhaps a Creole-spiked rich hollandaise makes them even better! **Serves 4.**

8–12	Alaskan jumbo king crab legs, 12" (30 cm) long, split lengthwise
2 bunches	fresh thyme
8	bay leaves
1/2 pound (250 grams)	unsalted butter, melted
2 tbsp. (30 mL)	olive oil
1 recipe	Creole Hollandaise (recipe follows) lemon wedges

Have ready 1/2 cup (125 mL) New Orleans Creole Sauce (page 39). Soak thyme leaves and bay leaves in warm water to cover 30 minutes, then drain. Prepare coals to medium-hot, about 45 minutes. Combine melted butter and olive oil.

Prepare Creole Hollandaise while coals are heating, and keep warm.

Oil grill, and place 4" (10 cm) from source of heat. Brush split sides of crab legs with butter-oil mixture. Scatter thyme branches and bay leaves over coals. Place crab legs on grill and sear 2–3 minutes. Brush with butter-oil and turn. Grill additional 2 minutes until lightly charred. Remove from grill to a large, warmed platter. Serve warm Creole Hollandaise as a dipping sauce for the hot grilled crab legs. Accompany with lemon wedges.

Creole Hollandaise

1/2 cup (125 mL)	New Orleans Creole Sauce (page 39)
1/2 pound (250 grams)	very fresh best-quality butter
3	egg yolks, at room temperature
1 tbsp. (15 mL)	water, at body temperature
1 tbsp. (15 mL)	grainy Creole-style mustard
1 tbsp. (15 mL)	lemon juice
1 tsp. (5 mL)	finely grated lemon rind salt freshly ground black pepper

Simmer the Creole Sauce in a small saucepan over low heat until reduced almost by half. Set aside. Melt the butter over low heat until completely liquid; remove from heat and set aside to cool down to just warm.

Place egg yolks and water in a food processor or blender. Beat on high until thickened and creamy (the thicker the yolks, the thicker the finished sauce will be). With the motor running, begin adding the warm butter, drop by drop at first, increasing the amount at the end. Discard white solids at bottom of pan. Finally, beat in the mustard, lemon juice and rind. Taste and correct for seasonings with salt and pepper. Transfer sauce to a crockery mixing bowl which has been rinsed out with warm water and dried. Whisk in the reduced Creole Sauce.

BARBECUED OYSTER ROAST

An authentic oyster roast is a grand celebration for oyster lovers! All you need is a smoky fire, bushels of fresh oysters and a few accompaniments. (And a gathering of friends who are afficionados of this delicious bivalve.) Serve with hot, crusty bread, coleslaw, and corn on the cob done on the grill.

1 dozen, or more	fresh oysters (for each person)
	salt and pepper
	Tabasco sauce
	melted butter (generous skillet full)
	lemon wedges
	cruet of malt vinegar

Scrub the oysters well. Heat coals to very hot, about 1 hour. Place oiled grill 3"–4" (7cm–10 cm) over coals. Place oysters, in small batches, directly on grill. Cover with hood, or a tent of heavy-duty foil, to keep the heat in. Watch oysters carefully—they are done precisely when they open, in 4–6 minutes.

Serve oysters hot, as they come off the grill. Continue to barbecue oysters until everyone has had enough. Each person seasons their oysters as they wish: with salt and pepper, with a dip in hot butter, with a squeeze of lemon, a dash of vinegar or a drop of Tabasco.

SUMMER PAELLA
WITH GRILLED SHELLFISH

Paella is a saffron-scented rice extravaganza, studded with chicken, shrimp, mussels and vegetables. Unless carefully timed, the delicate shellfish can be overcooked, so this method is ideal: the paella is prepared ahead of time and simmered to an ideal finish, while the shellfish grill separately. Serve with a cold gazpacho soup, to sip while the seafood is grilling, and accompany the main event with icy pitchers of fruit-laden Sangría. **Serves 6.**

6 tbsp. (45 mL)	Spanish olive oil
1 large	Spanish onion, peeled, halved and thinly sliced
2 large cloves	garlic, peeled and slivered
1 *each* large	red, green and yellow bell pepper, stemmed, seeded and thinly sliced
1/2 tsp. (2 mL)	saffron, pulverized
2 tsp. (10 mL)	imported Hungarian or Spanish paprika
1 tsp. (5 mL)	sugar
1 tsp. (5 mL)	thyme leaves
4 ripe	tomatoes, skinned, seeded and coarsely chopped
2 cups (500 mL)	rice, preferably Italian *arborio* style (may substitute a short, chewy grain)
2 tsp. (10 mL)	salt
3 1/2 cups (875 mL)	rich chicken stock
	Grilled Shellfish (recipe follows)
	lemon wedges and parsley, as garnish

In an over-sized paella pan or skillet, heat the olive oil over medium-high heat. Add the onions and sauté 4–5 minutes until softened. Add the garlic and sauté 1–2 minutes. Add the sliced bell peppers, reduce heat to medium and cook until softened and just lightly colored.

Stir in the saffron, paprika, sugar and thyme. Sauté 2 minutes to blend thoroughly. Stir in the tomatoes, increase heat to high and cook, stirring 4–5 minutes until juices are absorbed.

Stir in the rice, salt and chicken stock and bring mixture to a simmer. Reduce heat to medium-low and partially cover. Simmer 25–30 minutes, or just until rice is tender. Remove from heat and allow paella to rest 15 minutes before topping with hot grilled seafood and serving. Garnish with lemon wedges and parsley.

Grilled Shellfish

1/2 cup (125 mL)	Spanish olive oil
2 cloves	garlic, peeled and minced
1 tbsp. (15 mL)	imported Hungarian or Spanish paprika
1 pound (500 grams)	large shrimp (prawns), shelled, deveined, tails intact; threaded on skewers
1 pound (500 grams)	fresh sea scallops; threaded on skewers
2 pounds (1 kg)	fresh mussels, scrubbed thoroughly in cold water
2 pounds (1 kg)	fresh clams, scrubbed thoroughly in cold water

Prepare coals to medium-hot, about 45 minutes. Place grill 4" (10 cm) above source of heat. In a small saucepan, heat olive oil, garlic, paprika and lemon juice 1 minute. Whisk smooth, and set aside to cool to room temperature.

Oil grill. Brush skewered shrimp and scallops with flavored oil, and turn to cook 2 minutes on other side. Remove from grill. Place closed mussels and clams directly on grill and cook just until they open. Brush with any remaining oil and remove from grill. Break off and discard the empty half of each shell.

GRILLED FRESH CLAMS WITH AÏOLI

Fresh clams, washed and soaked in cold water one hour before grilling, make for easy entertaining and simple cleanup. Provide a big bucket for the empty shells, and large checkered napkins to tuck under chins. Serve with a crock of garlicky Aïoli for dipping. Serves 6–8.

6 pounds (3 kg)	fresh clams in their shells (select Eastern steamers, quahogs, littlenecks and cherrystones *or* westcoast razor clams, pismo or littlenecks)
1 recipe	Aïoli (page 40)

Scrub the clam shells well, and soak in 3–4 changes of ice-cold, fresh salted water. This will force the clams to give up any sand or grit. All shells should be intact, not broken or cracked, and should feel heavy.

Heat coals to red hot, about 45 minutes. Lightly oil grill. Place scrubbed clams directly on grill and cook until clams open wide. Discard any clams which refuse to open. Cooking time will be about 3–5 minutes. Remove clams, as they open, to a large platter, and serve with a chilled crock of Aïoli for dipping.

POULTRY ON THE GRILL

A simple baste with olive oil and herbs does chicken on the grill to a beautiful finish, or good, prepared barbecue sauce slathered on during the final minutes on the grill makes it irresistible. But these recipes go one step further, giving you chicken in a "drunken" sauce heady with beer, chicken glazed with a Port- and orange-spiked Cumberland sauce, chicken done tandoori style with marinade of spicy yogurt. But don't restrict yourself to chicken when you're grilling. Game hens also grill beautifully—whether done over mesquite with herbs or glazed "Canadian-style" with a buttery maple syrup glaze. Try duck breast marinated in a citrus-and-sage bath and accompanied by grilled apples. And turkey has come out of the oven—and onto the barbecue—as a whole breast with a pungent mustard-butter, as fruit-laced kebabs or as thick grilled steaks in a lemony glaze.

CHICKEN IN DRUNKEN BARBECUE SAUCE

This is one of the simplest and most delicious recipes in the book. Use your favorite bottled barbecue sauce (smoky-flavored or not) and add butter and beer. That's it! You've never tasted chicken off the grill as good as this! Serve with buttery garlic bread, fresh tomato salad and corn on the cob. Ice-cold beer is the obvious beverage. Serves 4.

3 pounds (1.5 kg)	meaty chicken, cut up
1/4 pound (125 grams)	butter, melted
14-ounce (400-gram) bottle	barbecue sauce
12-ounce (375-mL) bottle	lager, or ale
4 tbsp. (60 mL)	butter
4 tbsp. (60 mL)	vegetable oil

Combine the melted butter, barbecue sauce and beer in a heavy, deep saucepan over medium heat. Simmer 5 minutes, stirring and set aside.

Melt remaining 4 tbsp. (60 mL) *each* butter and oil. Brush over chicken pieces. Lightly oil grill. Place chicken pieces over coals 6" (15 cm) from heat source. Grill 5 minutes on each side before brushing with barbecue sauce. Season with salt and pepper.

Continue grilling chicken, brushing generously with sauce, 35–45 minutes, or until meat just tests tender and skin is a rich brown with char marks. Transfer chicken to a platter, allow to sit 5–7 minutes and serve. Pass any remaining sauce for dipping.

CHICKEN BREASTS PROVENÇAL

Try these chicken breasts done over hot coals perfumed with a scattering of dried, aromatic herbes de provençe (available in the dried herb section; a special mixture of dried rosemary, oregano, thyme, basil, fennel seed and lavender). The marinade is tart, with the bite of citrus, garlic, olive oil and additional herbs. Serve with fresh haricot vert, polenta baked with Parmesan, a dry French Rosé nicely chilled, and a hot, crusty baguette with a crock of sweet butter. **Serves 4–6.**

4 whole	chicken breasts, skin and bones attached, cracked at the breastbone and flattened out
1 recipe	Provençal Marinade (page 15)
3 tbsp. (45 mL)	dried herbes de provençe
	lemon wedges
	bunches of fresh herbs or lavender, as garnish

Place flattened chicken breasts in a glass casserole and cover with prepared Provençal Marinade, turning to coat. Marinate at room temperature 2–3 hours, turning several times.

Prepare coals to ashen white, about 1 hour. Place grill 4" (10 cm) over coals. Oil grill and scatter the dried herbs directly over coals. Remove breasts from marinade and place on grill skin-side down. Sear 3–4 minutes, turn and sear additional side. Continue to grill, brushing with marinade frequently, until breasts are just tender at thickest part and skin is a rich golden brown with slight charring. Total grilling time will be about 20–25 minutes.

Remove breasts from grill and allow to rest 10 minutes for juices to be absorbed. Cut each breast in half, through the backbone. Place on a large, country-style platter, garnish with lemon wedges and sprigs of fresh herbs, and serve warm or at room temperature.

CHICKEN BREASTS WITH TARRAGON AND ORANGE-CURRY MUSTARD MARINADE

Plump, meaty, chicken breasts are wonderful flavored with tarragon and this snappy marinade of orange, curry and two mustards. Grill to a nicely charred finish, and accompany with a crock of French grainy mustard, a crisp baguette, sweet butter and a salad of curly endive, crisp bacon, and garlic croutons. Serves 4–6.

4 whole	boneless chicken breasts, skin attached
1 recipe	Orange-Curry Mustard Marinade (page 20)
8 sprigs	fresh tarragon
1	orange, cut in half
	salt
	freshly ground black pepper
1/3 cup (75 mL)	dried tarragon leaves
	orange wedges or slices
	crisp sprigs fresh tarragon, as garnish

Carefully loosen the skin of each chicken breast to form a pocket on each half of either side of the breast-bone area. Gently slip a generous sprig of fresh tarragon into each pocket. Press skin flat to seal. Rub each whole breast, on both sides, with the cut orange, and season with salt and pepper. Allow to marinate at room temperature while preparing coals.

Prepare coals to medium-hot, about 45 minutes. Place grill 6" (15 cm) above coals. Scatter dried tarragon over coals. Place chicken breasts skin-side down on grill and sear 3 minutes. Turn and sear other side 3 minutes. Continue to grill, basting with prepared Orange-Curry Mustard Marinade on both sides until breasts are tender and skin is a rich, golden brown. Total cooking time will be about 20–22 minutes.

Remove grilled breasts and allow to rest 15 minutes. Cut each breast in half along the breastbone with a sharp chef's knife. Each piece should have a "picture window" with the sprig of tarragon showing through the skin. Place on a country-style platter, garnish with fresh tarragon and wedges or slices of orange. Serve warm or at room temperature.

BARBECUED CHICKEN LEGS HOISIN

Look for Chinese Hoisin sauce in the Oriental section of your supermarket. It is a heady paste-like sauce of soybeans, garlic and fragrant Chinese spices. Serve these chicken legs with stir-fried snow peas topped with toasted sesame seeds, steamed brown or white rice and the accompanying grilled onions and pineapple. **Serves 6.**

6 meaty	chicken leg-thigh portions
10-ounce (300 mL) bottle	Chinese Hoisin sauce
2 tbsp. (30 mL)	Sherry vinegar *or* rice wine vinegar
1 tbsp. (15 mL)	dry Sherry or Scotch whiskey
2 tbsp. (30 mL)	peanut oil
3 tbsp. (45 mL)	minced scallions
	additional vinegar
	salt and freshly ground pepper
1 fresh	pineapple, top and bottom removed, rind removed; cut into 6 wedges, top to bottom
2 large	red onions, peeled, top and bottom slice removed and sliced into thirds, horizontally
	additional minced scallions, as garnish

Combine the hoisin sauce, vinegar, Sherry or Scotch, peanut oil and minced scallions in a small, heavy saucepan. Heat 3–4 minutes over very low heat, stirring, until mixture simmers. Remove from heat.

Brush chicken portions with vinegar on both sides and season with salt and pepper. Allow to marinate at room temperature while preparing coals.

Prepare coals to medium-hot, about 45 minutes. Place grill 4"–6" (10 cm–15 cm) above source of heat. Place chicken, skin-side down, on oiled grilled and sear 3–4 minutes. Turn and sear other side 3–4 minutes. Continue to grill chicken, basting with hoisin mixture, until chicken is tender and skin is a glossy, rich, golden brown, about 20–25 minutes total cooking time.

While chicken is grilling, place pineapple and onions around outer perimeter of grill. Brush with sauce and grill 3–4 minutes per side, until nicely browned and just tender.

Remove chicken and grilled fruit and onions to a large platter. Allow to rest 10 minutes before serving. Sprinkle with minced scallions and serve warm.

CUMBERLAND-GRILLED CHICKEN

Classic Cumberland Sauce is a great glaze for grilled chicken. This recipe is delicious on tiny baby chickens (poussins) that have been split open and butterflied. The marinade may be prepared several days in advance and stored in the refrigerator. This sauce is also delectable on turkey. **Serves 4.**

4 1-pound (500-gram)	chickens, split open down the back and butterflied flat
1	orange, cut in half
1	lemon, cut in half
	salt
	cayenne pepper
	orange and lemon zest, as garnish
1 recipe	Cumberland Sauce for Grilling (recipe follows)

Prepare the Cumberland Sauce, cool completely and set aside until ready to use.

Bring the chickens to room temperature and rub with cut orange and lemon on both sides. Season liberally with salt and cayenne pepper. Allow to marinate while preparing coals to medium-hot, about 45 minutes. Place grill 6" (15 cm) above coals. Oil grill.

Place chickens flat on grill, skin-side down and sear 5 minutes. Turn and sear other side. Begin basting with sauce, and continue to grill until chickens are tender and skin is glazed a rich golden brown, 25–30 minutes total.

Remove chickens from grill, place on warmed plates and garnish with orange and lemon zest. Serve at once.

Cumberland Sauce for Grilling

1 cup (250 mL)	red currant jelly
1/3 cup (75 mL)	Port
1 tbsp. (15 mL)	red wine vinegar
1 small	orange, ground (including rind)
2 tbsp. (30 mL)	fresh lemon juice
	grated zest from 1 lemon
1 tbsp. (15 mL)	Dijon mustard
1/2 tsp. (2 mL)	ground ginger
3" (7 cm)	cinnamon stick
1	bay leaf
1/4 tsp. (1 mL) *each*	salt and pepper
	pinch ground cloves

Combine all ingredients in a small, stainless steel saucepan and bring to a simmer over low heat. Cook sauce, stirring, until jelly is completely melted, and sauce simmers 4 5 minutes. Cool sauce to room temperature before using.

YAKITORI CHICKEN KEBABS

These chicken kebabs are marinated in a wash of soy sauce, Mirin (Japanese sweet rice wine), sugar and ginger, and threaded on bamboo skewers with colorful green scallions and red, yellow and green bell peppers. Serve with steamed white rice and ice-cold Japanese beer. Place grilled kebabs on a serving platter lined with large fresh leaves for a distinctive Japanese touch. Makes 1 dozen skewers. Serves 6.

12	bamboo skewers, 10" (25 cm) long, soaked in warm water 45 minutes and drained
3 pounds (1.5 kg)	boneless chicken breast, skin attached, cut into 1 1/4" (3 cm) cubes (partially frozen breasts make cutting easier)
1 *each* large	red, green and yellow bell pepper; stemmed, seeded and cut into 1" (2.5 cm) squares
2 bunches	green scallions, cut into 2" (5 cm) lengths (use white and tender green sections only)
1 medium-sized	fresh pineapple, cubed
1 recipe	Yakitori Marinade (recipe follows)

Thread the chicken cubes on soaked bamboo skewers alternating with peppers, scallions and pineapple. Prepare Yakitori Marinade several hours before using, to allow flavors to blend. Place threaded kebabs in marinade for 15 minutes at room temperature, turning frequently.

Prepare coals to medium-hot, about 45 minutes. Place grill 4" (10 cm) from coals and brush with oil. Remove kebabs from marinade, and place on grill. Sear 2 minutes on each side and continue to grill, basting with marinade. Total cooking time will be about 8 minutes, or just until chicken is tender, opaque and nicely charred on outside. Do not overcook. Remove from grill and serve at once.

Heat any remaining marinade in a small saucepan and reduce over high heat until syrupy. Drizzle, if desired, over grilled kebabs.

Yakitori Marinade

1/2 cup (125 mL)	soy sauce
1/2 cup (125 mL)	Japanese sweet rice wine (available in Oriental sections of the supermarket)
1/3 cup (75 mL)	peanut oil
2 large cloves	garlic, peeled and crushed
2 tbsp. (30 mL)	brown sugar, packed
2 tbsp. (30 mL)	grated fresh ginger

Whisk all ingredients together until smooth and well combined. Set aside 3–4 hours before using to blend flavors.

INDIAN TEKKA CHICKEN KEBABS

Chicken done on a skewer with a pungent yogurt marinade flavored with fragrant spices is a real treat. Serve with a fresh cucumber and mint salad, saffron rice studded with dates and almonds, and assorted chutneys. **Serves 4–6.**

3 pounds (1.5 kg)	boneless chicken breasts and thighs, skin attached, cut into 2" (5 cm) cubes
3	purple onions, peeled and quartered, and separated into sections 4 layers thick
1 1/2 cups (375 mL)	plain unflavored yogurt
2 large cloves	garlic, peeled and pressed
2 tbsp. (30 mL)	finely grated fresh ginger
1 tsp. (5 mL) *each*	ground coriander, curry powder, cinnamon and black pepper
2 tbsp. (30 mL)	fresh lemon juice
2 tsp. (10 mL)	finely grated lemon rind
1 tsp. (5 mL) *each*	ground chili powder and salt
8 tbsp. (125 mL)	butter, melted
1/2 cup (125 mL)	scallions, sliced paper-thin
	lemon wedges

Thread chicken cubes alternately with onion pieces on skewers. Place skewers in a rectangular baking dish long enough that skewers will lie down flat.

Whisk together the yogurt, garlic, ginger, spices, lemon juice, rind, chili powder and salt. Pour over skewers, turn and coat all sides evenly. Cover and refrigerate 3 hours, turning skewers once.

Bring chicken to room temperature while preparing coals to ashen white, about 1 hour. Place grill 4" (10 cm) above source of heat.

Generously oil grill. Remove skewers from marinade and place on grill. Grill skewers 4–5 minutes per side, brushing with melted butter. Finished skewers should be a rich, golden brown, and the chicken should be just tender. Do not overcook. Remove from grill and place skewers on a large platter. Sprinkle with sliced scallions, garnish with lemon wedges, and serve at once.

Opposite: Chicken in Drunken Barbecue Sauce, Grilled Fresh Corn with Garlic and Herbed Lemon Butter, Best-Ever Garlic Bread, Beefsteak Tomatoes in Fresh Basil Vinaigrette.

BARBECUED TANDOORI CHICKEN

A wonderful marinade of yogurt and exotic spices transforms this chicken into a juicy, tangy-crusted flavor treat. Serve with warm chapatis (Indian breads), a fresh vegetable salad, rice pilaf and assorted fruit chutneys. **Serves 4.**

3-pound (1500-gram)	broiler chicken, quartered
2 cups (500 mL)	unflavored yogurt
1 medium-sized	lemon, ground (including rind)
1 tsp. (5 mL) *each*	curry powder, ground ginger, ground cumin, ground allspice, ground cinnamon
3 large cloves	garlic, peeled and pressed
1 tbsp. (15 mL)	imported paprika
1 tsp. (5 mL)	salt
1/2 tsp. (2 mL)	cayenne pepper
	lemon wedges
	fresh cilantro (Chinese parsley, fresh coriander)
	finely diced red onion

Slash the chicken on skin-side in 1/4"-deep (1/2 cm) diagonal stripes 1" (2.5 cm) apart. Whisk together the yogurt, ground lemon, spices, garlic, paprika, salt and cayenne. Place chicken in a bowl and cover on all sides with the marinade. Cover and chill 6–8 hours, turning chicken twice.

Prepare coals to ashen white, about 1 hour. Bring chicken to room temperature while preparing coals. Place grill 6" (15 cm) above source of heat. Generously oil grill.

Place chicken, skin-side down, on grill and cook 10–15 minutes until golden brown, basting with marinade. Turn, continue to baste and cook additional 15–18 minutes, or until chicken is just tender and crust is a rich, golden brown. Remove from grill to a large platter.

Sprinkle chicken with diced onion, surround with lemon wedges and cilantro. Serve immediately.

JAMBALAYA WITH BARBECUED CHICKEN AND SAUSAGE

Prepare this simple version of Jambalaya ahead of time, grill the chicken and sausage separately, and add just before serving. Serve with a crisp green salad, bottles of ice-cold lager and crusty garlic bread. **Serves 6.**

3-pound (1500-gram)	fryer chicken, cut into serving pieces (or 6 leg portions and 6 thigh portions, if desired)
1 1/2 pounds (750 grams)	smoked sausage (such as kielbasa, Cajun andouille or other spicy, cooked sausage)
1 tbsp. (15 mL) *each*	paprika, celery salt, black pepper, sugar
1/2 cup (125 mL)	olive oil
	lemon and lime wedges
1 recipe	Jambalaya (recipe follows)

Prepare the Jambalaya 1–3 hours before serving. Bring chicken pieces to room temperature. Combine the paprika, celery salt, black pepper and sugar, and rub on both sides of chicken pieces. Let chicken "dry marinate" 45 minutes while preparing coals. Slice sausage into 3" (7 cm) lengths, cut on the diagonal. Score sausages very lightly on both sides.

Prepare coals to medium-hot, about 45 minutes. Place grill 4" (10 cm) over coals. Oil grill. Place chicken, skin-side down, on grill and sear 2 minutes. Turn and sear other side. Place sausages around outer perimeter of grill and cook until slightly charred on both sides and heated completely through. Brush chicken pieces with olive oil and continue to grill 5–6 minutes on each side until tender and a rich, golden brown. Remove chicken and sausage pieces from grill and place on prepared Jambalaya, tucking into rice part way. Garnish with lemon and lime wedges and serve at once.

Jambalaya

6 slices	smoked bacon, diced
6 tbsp. (90 mL)	olive oil
1 cup (250 mL) *each*	chopped onion, scallions, celery and green bell pepper
3 cloves	garlic, peeled and chopped
3	bay leaves, crumbled
2 tsp. (10 mL)	dried thyme leaves
1 tbsp. (15 mL)	paprika
1/2 tsp. (2 mL)	cayenne pepper
2 tsp. (10 mL)	salt
2 cups (500 mL)	long-grain rice
12-ounce (375 mL) can	beer at room temperature
12 ounces (375 mL)	chicken stock

In a large, deep cast-iron Dutch oven, lightly brown the bacon over medium-high heat, stirring. Add the olive oil and heat 2 minutes. Stir in the chopped vegetables and continue to sauté, stirring until vegetables are light golden brown. Add the garlic, bay leaves, thyme, paprika, cayenne and salt. Increase heat to high and sauté mixture 2–3 minutes until glossy.

Add the raw rice and stir over high heat until completely coated with oil. Stir in the beer and stock, bring to a boil, reduce heat to low and simmer partially covered until rice is tender and liquid is absorbed. Do not stir. Cooking time will be 20–30 minutes.

Remove Jambalaya from heat, and allow to stand 10 minutes covered with a clean cloth towel. Fluff with a long-pronged fork. Top with hot, grilled chicken and sausage and serve at once.

MESQUITE-GRILLED GAME HENS

Cornish game hens are great for entertaining—each is a perfect size for a generous serving. Try the tender little hens this way—and enjoy their smoky, slightly charred flavor. Serve with wild rice tossed with toasted pecans and chopped dates, and a salad of curly chicory with red onion and thin slices of fresh oranges. **Serves 4.**

4	Cornish game hens, fresh (or frozen and defrosted), each 1 pound (500 grams),
2/3 cup (150 mL)	olive oil
3 tbsp. (45 mL)	fresh lemon juice
2 cloves	garlic, peeled and pressed
4 tbsp. (60 mL)	hot melted butter
1 tbsp. (15 mL) *each*	dried rosemary, and thyme leaves, crumbled
	salt
	freshly ground black pepper
	fresh sprigs of rosemary, as garnish

With a sharp knife, split each hen down the backbone. Press the breast-bones firmly, so that they lie completely flat. Tuck wings under in a flat position.

Whisk together the olive oil, lemon juice, garlic, hot melted butter, and rosemary and thyme leaves. Brush mixture over both sides of each flattened hen. Marinate at room temperature for 1 hour, skin side up.

Soak 8–10 mesquite chips in warm water to cover for 30 minutes; drain. Lightly oil grill, and place 6" (15 cm) above medium-hot coals. Place drained mesquite chips directly on coals.

Place hens on oiled grill, skin-side down. Basting with marinade, cook hens about 8 minutes on each side, turning once. Skin should be crisped and slightly charred, and meat should *just* feel slightly firmed when pressed. Legs should move freely in the joint. Season with salt and pepper on both sides during final 2 minutes of grilling.

Serve on warmed, oversized plates, garnished with rosemary.

MAPLE-GLAZED GAME HENS

This delicious amber liquid makes a wonderful base for a buttery, lemon- and Bourbon-spiked glaze, perfect on split game hens. Serve with tiny carrots braised in butter, fresh peas, wild rice and hot, yeasty, home-baked rolls with a crock of sweet butter. Hard cider, nicely chilled, is the perfect beverage.
Serves 4.

4 1-pound (500-gram)	fresh Rock Cornish game hens, rinsed and patted dry
2	lemons, halved
4 tsp. (20 mL)	dried thyme leaves
1 recipe	Maple Syrup Glaze (page 38)
	salt
	pepper
	fresh maple leaves, wiped clean, as garnish
	lemon slices

Prepare the Maple Syrup Glaze and set aside. Split each game hen open by cutting along the backbone. Pull hens open, place on flat surface and press flat (cracking backbone, if needed) to butterfly hens. Rub with cut lemons on both sides, and sprinkle with dried thyme leaves. Allow to stand at room temperature while preparing coals.

Prepare coals to medium-hot, about 45 minutes. Place grill 4"–6" (10 cm–15 cm) above coals. Place hens on oiled grill, skin-side down, and sear 8 minutes. Season with salt and pepper and turn over. Sear 8 minutes and season with salt and pepper. Begin brushing hens with prepared glaze, turning and grilling additional 12–14 minutes until hens are tender, and skin is highly glazed and golden brown. Remove hens from grill to a large platter and allow to rest 10 minutes before serving.

If desired, heat any remaining glaze and drizzle over hens. Garnish with fresh maple leaves and vines, and tuck in fresh lemon slices. Serve at once.

CORNISH GAME HENS
WITH PUNGENT RASPBERRY GLAZE

Split game hens, or tiny poussins (baby chickens) done on the grill with this wonderful raspberry glaze make the loveliest of summertime entertaining fare. Serve with stir-fried spinach and wild rice, and garnish with fresh vine or raspberry leaves and a few scattered fresh raspberries. **Serves 4.**

4 1-pound (500-gram)	Cornish game hens (or *poussins*), split in half
2/3 cup (150 mL)	raspberry vinegar
1/3 cup (75 mL)	red wine vinegar
2 large cloves	garlic, peeled and pressed
3	bay leaves, crumbled
2 tbsp. (30 mL)	minced shallots
2/3 cup (150 mL)	puréed fresh raspberries
1 tsp. (5 mL)	dried thyme leaves
1 tsp. (5 mL)	cracked black peppercorns
1/2 cup (125 mL)	olive oil
10 sprigs	fresh thyme soaked in warm water 20 minutes, and drained
8	bay leaves soaked in warm water 20 minutes, and drained
	fresh vine leaves or large raspberry leaves
	fresh whole raspberries
	fresh thyme (with flowers) and fresh bay leaves (optional garnish)

Whisk together the vinegars, garlic, bay leaves, shallots, raspberry purée, thyme and cracked pepper. Slowly whisk in the olive oil in a thin, steady steam until mixture is smooth. Place split birds in a glass casserole and over with marinade, turning to coat. Cover and refrigerate 4–5 hours, turning several times to coat birds.

Bring hens to room temperature while heating coals to medium-hot, about 45 minutes. Place grill 4"–6" (10 cm–15 cm) above source of heat. Oil grill. Scatter drained thyme sprigs and bay leaves over coals.

Remove birds from marinade and place on grill, skin-side down. Sear 3–4 minutes, turn and sear other side. Continue to grill, basting with marinade, until just tender (leg will move easily when wiggled), and skin is a glossy, caramelized golden brown. Do not overcook. Total cooking time will be about 25 minutes.

Heat any remaining marinade until reduced to about 4 tbsp. (60 mL) and thickened. Remove grilled birds and place on oversized plates. Tuck fresh leaves partially under birds as garnish. Nap with 1 tbsp. (15 mL) sauce and scatter with 4–5 fresh raspberries. Serve hot or warm, garnished with sprigs of fresh thyme and bay leaves (if desired).

SOUTHWEST GLAZED GAME HENS

*These spicy glazed game hens are simple to prepare, beautiful to serve and make a most unusual dish for entertaining. Serve with hot cornbread, grilled corn and Smoky Baked Black Beans. You'll find the jalapeño jelly in the specialty section of your supermaket. **Serves 4.***

4 1-pound (500-gram)	fresh Rock Cornish game hens, rinsed and patted dry
2	limes, halved
	freshly ground black pepper
8-ounce (250-mL) jar	jalapeño jelly (green or red variety)
3 tbsp. (45 mL)	fresh lime juice
1 tbsp. (15 mL)	finely grated lemon rind
6 tbsp. (90 mL)	butter
	large fresh green leaves, as garnish under hens
	fresh cilantro (fresh coriander, Chinese parsley)
	lime wedges

Split each game hen open by cutting along backbone. Pull hens open, place on a flat work surface and press flat (cracking backbone, if needed) to "butterfly" hens. Rub hens with cut limes on both sides and sprinkle liberally with black pepper. Allow to stand at room temperature while preparing glaze and coals.

While preparing coals to medium-hot, about 45 minutes, prepare jelly glaze. Melt jelly over low heat in a small saucepan, and stir in the lime juice, rind and butter. Simmer until butter is melted and mixture bubbles. Remove from heat and set aside. Keep warm until ready to use.

Place grill 4"–6" (10 cm–15 cm) above coals. Oil grill. Place hens on grill, skin-side down, and sear 8 minutes. Turn and sear remaining side 8 minutes. Begin brushing with warm jelly glaze, turning and grilling additional 12–14 minutes until hens are tender and skin is a highly glazed and golden brown. Remove hens from grill, place on large platter and allow to rest 10 minutes before serving. Season with salt.

Heat any remaining glaze and serve with hens. Garnish with fresh cilantro and lime wedges. (This dish is especially pretty if the grilled hens are presented on rustic plates lined with a single, large leaf or fresh lemon leaves. A single tropical blosson tucked in is a pretty addition.)

GRILLED DUCK BREASTS
WITH CITRUS AND SAGE MARINADE
AND GRILLED APPLES

This is a superb way of preparing duck breasts, first marinated in a pungent bath of olive oil, fresh lemon, orange and sage, then char-grilled over coals with the added aroma of fresh sage. Serve with plump grilled apples, crispy shoe-string potatoes and a tart salad of radicchio and curly endive. **Serves 6.**

6 large	meaty duck breasts, boned
1 recipe	Citrus and Sage Marinage (page 15)
1 bunch	fresh sage, soaked in warm water 15 minutes, drained
	salt
	freshly ground black pepper
4	tart green apples, cored, top and bottom slice removed
4 tbsp. (60 mL)	butter, melted
	long, thin, lemon-zest "curls"
	fresh sage leaves, as garnish

Prepare Citrus and Sage Marinade, add duck breasts, cover and refrigerate 12 hours or overnight. Turn breasts several times.

Bring duck breasts and marinade to room temperature 45 minutes before grilling. Prepare coals to medium-hot, about 45 minutes. Place drained sage leaves directly on coals. Lightly oil grill, and place 6" (15 cm) above coals. Place duck breasts, skin-side down, on oiled grill and sear quickly, 2–3 minutes on each side. Salt and pepper to taste. Continue to grill breasts, moving them to indirect heat *or* cover grill and continue to cook until crisp and slightly charred on the outside and juicy pink inside—about 8–10 minutes per side. Continue to baste breasts with marinade during cooking. Remove breasts to a carving board, and allow to rest 5–7 minutes while grilling apples.

Add melted butter to remainder of marinade, and brush over apple-rings. Grill apples on an oiled grill until tender, 2–3 minutes per side. Brush with butter marinade during cooking time.

Slice each duck breast on the diagonal into 5 slices, place on warmed plates and serve garnished with grilled apple rings. Serve, if desired, with any of the savory flavored butters in this book.

GRILLED TURKEY BREAST
WITH CRISP BACON
AND DOUBLE-MUSTARD BUTTER

Turkey is such a wonderful meat that it is a shame to have it but a few times around festive holidays. Try this breast, marinated in an apple- and Port-flavored marinade, grilled over hot coals perfumed with applewood chips and served with rashers of bacon and a pungent slather of mustard butter. Serves 4. (This recipe calls for half a turkey breast, serving 4. A whole turkey breast will serve 8. The amount of marinade and flavored butter remains the same.)

2 3/4 pound (1375 gram)	half turkey breast
1 recipe	Port and Apple Marinade (page 16)
8 thick slices	smoky bacon, rind removed
2 cups (500 mL)	applewood chips, soaked 30 minutes in warm water and drained
1 recipe	Double-Mustard Butter (page 24) fresh sage, thyme and rosemary, as garnish

Prepare marinade according to directions. Place turkey breast in a glass or crockery casserole and cover with marinade. Cover and marinate 24 hours in the refrigerator, turning several times.

Bring turkey and marinade to room temperature while coals are heating to medium-hot, about 1 hour. Lightly oil grill. Remove turkey breast from marinade and pat dry. Sprinkle soaked and drained applewood chips directly on hot coals. Place turkey on grill, skin-side down, and grill until seared and golden on one side. Turn breast to sear other side. Begin basting with marinade and cook until internal temperature *just* reaches 160°F. (75°C.), about 25–35 minutes. Skin should be crisped and slightly charred and meat should be juicy and moist. Do not overcook. Season with salt and pepper.

Remove turkey breast to warmed platter; let rest 10–15 minutes before carving. Lightly re-oil grill and place bacon strips on grill. Cook until lightly crisped on both sides, turning once with tongs. Bring flavored butter to room temperature.

Carve turkey breast vertically, so that each slice is ringed with crisped skin. Serve several slices per serving on warmed plates, each topped with a piece of Double-Mustard Butter and 2 slices of hot, crisp bacon. Garnish with fresh sage, thyme or rosemary.

GRILLED TURKEY AND FRUIT KEBABS WITH SPICY CRANBERRY GLAZE

These beautiful glazed, grilled skewers of turkey, fresh pineapple and onions make lovely holiday or entertaining fare. Serve with a casserole of herb-flecked bread dressing, fresh broccoli with lemon-butter and crispy almonds, and a leafy green salad. **Serves 6.**

3 pounds (1500 grams)	boned turkey thigh, skin attached
1/4 pound (125 grams)	butter, melted
1/3 cup (75 mL)	dry sherry
1/3 cup (75 mL)	fresh orange juice
1 tsp. (5 mL) *each*	paprika and dried thyme leaves
1 3-pound (1500-gram)	fresh pineapple
2	purple onions, peeled and quartered, blanched in simmering water 2 minutes, drained and cooled
1 recipe	Spicy Cranberry Glaze (page 41) single flower blossoms and a pretty leaf, if available, for garnish

Melt the butter with the sherry, orange juice, paprika and thyme leaves. Simmer 2–3 minutes, remove from heat and cool completely.

Partially freeze turkey to firm meat slightly for ease in cubing, then cut into 1 1/2" (4 cm) cubes, leaving skin attached when possible. Toss cubed turkey with the cooled marinade and set aside at room temperature for 1 hour while preparing coals to medium-hot.

Prepare the Spicy Cranberry Glaze and set aside. Soak wooden bamboo skewers in warm water 30 minutes (to prevent burning on the grill); then drain. Steam and peel the fresh pineapple; cube pineapple flesh into 2" (5 cm) cubes.

Place oiled grill 4"–6" (10 cm–15 cm) above coals. Remove turkey from marinade. Thread on long bamboo skewers, alternating with pineapple cubes and several slices of onion, beginning and ending with turkey. Place skewers on grill and cook, turning every 3–4 minutes to brown. Begin basting with glaze, brushing and turning, until turkey is golden brown and just tender—about 12–15 minutes total cooking time. Season at end of cooking time with salt and pepper.

Place grilled skewers on plates or a platter lined with fresh leaves. Garnish, if desired, with orchids or pretty single blossoms. Serve with any remaining sauce.

LEMON-GLAZED TURKEY STEAKS

Turkey has become a year-round favorite, no longer confined to the holiday table. Low in fat, high in protein, turkey is an ideal meat for the health-conscious '80s. These quickly grilled turkey steaks, with their sherry-spiked lemon glaze are great with grilled yams, pears, and melon wedges, hot wild rice, steamed fresh asparagus, and a crisp green salad. Add a bottle of icy Chardonnay for a perfect meal. **Serves 6.**

6 8-ounce (250-gram)	turkey breast "steaks," 3/4" (2 cm) thick
1/4 pound (125 grams)	butter, melted
2 tbsp. (30 mL)	olive oil
1/3 cup (75 mL)	fresh lemon juice
3 tbsp. (45 mL)	soy sauce
3 tbsp. (45 mL)	brown sugar, packed
2 tsp. (10 mL)	dried rosemary leaves, crumbled
1 tbsp. (15 mL)	Dijon mustard
3 tbsp. (45 mL)	Sherry
1 recipe	Grilled Fruit Baste (recipe follows)
3 large	yams, peeled and halved *or* quartered lengthwise
3 firm	pears (such as Bosc), halved *or* quartered
6 wedges	melon (such as cantaloupe or honeydew)

Bring to a simmer the melted butter, olive oil, lemon juice, soy sauce, brown sugar, rosemary, Dijon mustard and Sherry. Simmer 1–2 minutes until bubbly, and remove from heat. Cool to room temperature.

Pour cooled marinade over turkey steaks and marinate at room temperature while preparing coals to hot, about 1 hour. Place grill 4" (10 cm) above coals and oil grill.

Remove turkey steaks from marinade and place on hot grill. Sear about 4–5 minutes per side, brushing with marinade, until golden brown with slightly crisped edges. Inside should be juicy and *just* no longer pink. Remove from grill and serve at once. Season with salt and pepper to taste. Discard marinade.

Serve turkey steaks hot, accompanied by the grilled vegetables and fruit.

Grilled Fruit Baste

6 tbsp. (90 mL)	butter, melted
2 tbsp. (30 mL)	oil
1 tsp. (5 mL)	dried rosemary *or* thyme leaves
	salt
	pepper

Combine the melted butter, oil and herbs. Heat 1 minute. Use to baste yam, pears and melon wedges over medium-hot coals, turning, until tender, nicely glazed and golden brown. Serve hot from the grill, seasoning with salt and pepper.

CHARCOAL-GRILLED CHICKEN BREASTS WITH DOUBLE-MUSTARD MARINADE

Try these zesty chicken breasts, done in minutes to a crusty turn on the grill, flavored with a double-mustard marinade spiked with brown sugar and old-fashioned cider vinegar. Serve with grilled corn, a crispy cole slaw, fresh summer tomatoes, and a great loaf of hot garlic bread. **Serves 6.**

6 medium-size whole	chicken breasts, boned
2 cloves	garlic, peeled and pressed
1 tsp. (5 mL)	salt
1/3 cup (75 mL)	light brown sugar, packed
1/3 cup (75 mL)	cider vinegar
1/4 cup (50 mL) *each*	grainy mustard and Dijon mustard
2 tsp. (10 mL)	dried thyme leaves
6 tbsp. (90 mL)	olive oil
	fresh watercress, washed and crisped

Place the chicken breasts flat in a shallow bowl. Whisk together the garlic, salt, brown sugar, vinegar, mustards, thyme leaves and olive oil, blending well. Pour over chicken, turning to coat. Refrigerate 6 hours, or overnight. Bring to room temperature, 1 hour, before grilling.

Prepare coals to ashen white, about 45 minutes. Place grill 4" (10 cm) above coals. Oil grill and heat. Remove breasts from marinade, and place on grill skin-side down. Sear 3–4 minutes. Turn and sear other side 4–6 minutes. Continue grilling, brushing with marinade for additional 5–7 minutes or until breasts are a rich, deep golden brown.

Remove chicken from grill, and allow to rest 10 minutes for juices to re-absorb. Using a very sharp chef's knife, slice each breast into thick diagonal slices. Serve, on warmed platters, on a bed of crisp watercress—one breast per portion.

GREAT GRILLING PARTNERS

Certain things just go together. Barbecued chicken and corn on the cob.
Grilled hamburgers and potato salad. Glazed pork spareribs and fresh
coleslaw. That's what this chapter is all about—twelve of this author's
favorite accompaniments—to get you started on your own. In this
chapter you'll find salads, instructions for grilling the world's best corn,
and earthy baked black beans. Baked items include hot corn muffins
flecked with red and green peppers and big, puffy herbed biscuits.
There's even a dessert to do right on the grill—savory baked apples
with a wonderful nutty filling, to enjoy with big scoops of vanilla ice
cream after the main event. Last but not least is a great recipe for garlic
bread—a barbecue must!

BEEFSTEAK TOMATOES
IN FRESH BASIL VINAIGRETTE

Serve this salad with just about anything hot off the grill. Make it in the summer when tomatoes are at their peak. If you are a gardener, then nothing is better than this salad made with your own home-grown tomatoes. ***Serves 6.***

4 large	firm-ripe beefsteak tomatoes, sliced into 1/4" (1/2 cm) rounds; about 3 generous cups (750 mL)
1/2 tsp. (2 mL)	salt
1 large clove	garlic, peeled and pressed
1/4 cup (50 mL)	fresh parsley leaves, packed
1/2 cup (125 mL)	fresh basil leaves, packed
1/2 tsp. (2 mL)	sugar
1/4 tsp. (1 mL)	coarsely ground black pepper
2 tbsp. (30 mL)	red wine vinegar
1/2 cup (125 mL)	olive oil

Arrange tomato slices in an overlapping circular pattern on a rimmed platter. In a food processor, purée the salt and garlic to a paste. Add the parsley and basil leaves and process to a grainy purée. Add the sugar, pepper and vinegar, and process until incorporated. With the motor running, add the olive oil in a thin, steady stream. Finished sauce should be a lovely green, thick vinaigrette. Pour dressing over tomatoes, allow salad to stand 15 minutes and serve cool.

Opposite: (Top to bottom) Greek Lamb Shish Kebabs, Seafood Brochettes with Savory Butter, Yakitori Chicken Kebabs.

PERFECT COLE SLAW

Fresh cabbage cole slaw is just about the perfect partner for anything hot off the barbecue grill. This is my favorite: simple, straightforward, nothing tricky— just plain, good, freshly made, old-fashioned cole slaw. **Serves 6–8.**

8 cups (2 litres)	fresh cabbage, cored and quartered and very finely shredded (select green cabbage, or a combination of both green and purple cabbage for a pretty effect)
1 cup (250 mL)	coarsely grated carrots (long shreds)
1/2 cup (125 mL)	minced onion *or* thinly sliced scallions
1 cup (250 mL)	best-quality mayonnaise
1/2 cup (125 mL)	sour cream, yogurt, or heavy cream
1 1/2 tsp. (7 mL)	whole celery seed
2 tbsp. (30 mL)	sugar
2 tbsp. (30 mL)	cider vinegar
	salt
	coarsely ground black peppercorns

Toss the cabbage, grated carrots and minced onion together in a large crockery bowl. Whisk together the mayonnaise, sour cream (or yogurt or heavy cream), celery seed, sugar and vinegar. Pour dressing over cabbage and toss gently to combine thoroughly. Season to taste with salt and pepper. Chill salad 1–3 hours, if desired, before serving. Serve chilled or cool.

BEST-EVER OLD-FASHIONED POTATO SALAD

What barbecue feast would be complete without potato salad! This is my favorite—nothing fancy, nothing nouvelle, nothing trendy—just good, old-fashioned ingredients, making a superb, hearty potato salad. **Serves 6.**

3 pounds (1500 grams)	potatoes (thin-skinned, new potatoes)
1 tbsp. (15 mL)	Dijon mustard
1 tsp. (5 mL)	sugar
3 tbsp. (45 mL)	apple cider vinegar
1/3 cup (75 mL)	light olive *or* safflower oil
	salt
	freshly ground coarse black pepper
1/3 cup (75 mL)	scallions, very thinly sliced
1 small	onion, peeled and finely minced
2/3 cup (150 mL)	tender celery stalks, finely chopped
1 cup (250 mL)	best-quality mayonnaise
1/3 cup (75 mL)	sour cream
2 tsp. (10 mL)	celery seed
6	hard-cooked eggs, chilled, peeled and coarsely chopped
	crisp greens or parsley
	paprika

Scrub the potatoes well. Place in a saucepan and cover with cold water. Partially cover pan, bring water to a soft boil and cook potatoes until just barely tender, about 18–20 minutes. Do not overcook. Drain potatoes and place on a kitchen towel until cool enough to handle. Peel warm potatoes, and cut into cubes into a large crockery bowl.

Whisk together the mustard, sugar, vinegar and oil. Pour over the warm potatoes and toss gently to coat. Season liberally with salt and pepper. Cover bowl and chill potatoes 3 hours.

Toss potatoes with the scallions, onion, celery, mayonnaise, sour cream and celery seed, tossing gently but thoroughly. Taste and correct for salt and pepper. Gently fold in the chopped hard-cooked eggs. Cover, and chill several hours (or overnight) before serving. Serve salad on a bed of crisp greens, with a garnish of parsley. Sprinkle with paprika, for a bit of color.

TWO GREAT WAYS WITH RICE: HERBED AND WILD

*Rice is a great partner for anything done on the grill—fish, poultry, ribs or steaks. Here are two, a classic white rice flecked with herbs and a wild rice studded with mushrooms and scallions. **Each recipe serves 4.***

Fresh Herbed White Rice

4 tbsp. (60 mL)	butter
1 1/2 cups (375 mL)	long-grain white rice
1 tsp. (5 mL)	salt
3 cups (750 mL)	boiling water
2	scallions, thinly sliced
3 tbsp. (45 mL)	snipped fresh herbs (select and combine dillweed, basil, thyme, marjoram, chives)
1 tbsp. (15 mL)	minced fresh parsley
2 tsp. (10 mL)	finely grated lemon rind (yellow part only)
	freshly ground black pepper

Heat the butter in a large, heavy saucepan over medium heat until foamy. Stir in the rice and sauté 2–3 minutes until translucent. Add the salt and boiling water. Reduce heat to low, cover and cook rice about 25 minutes until water is absorbed and rice is light and fluffy. Remove from heat and let stand 5 minutes. Add the scallions, minced herbs, parsley and lemon rind and toss with a fork. Season to taste with pepper. Serve while hot.

Wild Rice with Mushrooms and Scallions

1 cup (250 mL)	wild rice
4 cups (1 litre)	water
1 tsp. (5 mL)	salt
4 tbsp. (60 mL)	butter
2 tbsp. (30 mL)	olive oil
4	scallions, thinly sliced
1 clove	garlic, peeled and pressed
2/3 cup (150 mL)	thinly sliced fresh mushrooms
	salt
	freshly ground black pepper
2 tbsp. (30 mL)	minced fresh parsley (optional)

Rinse the wild rice thoroughly under cold running water. Bring the water and salt to a boil in a heavy saucepan. Stir in the wild rice, reduce heat to a simmer and cover. Cook rice 40–45 minutes or until *just* tender (the kernels will pop open). Do not cook to a mushy state. Drain rice well in a fine sieve and set aside.

In a large skillet, heat the butter and oil over medium-high heat. Sauté the scallions, garlic and sliced mushrooms together 4–5 minutes, tossing, until just pale golden. Stir in the rice, heat through 2–3 minutes and season to taste with salt and pepper. Stir in minced parsley, if desired. Serve at once, hot.

GRILLED FRESH CORN

This is absolutely the most delicious method of preparing fresh corn on the cob. Freshness is the key—and "just picked" corn is the ticket here. Slather with any one of the flavored savory butters in the book for a real treat. **Serves 6.**

6 ears	very fresh corn
6 tbsp. (90 mL)	softened butter (or flavored butter)
	cold water
	additional butter or flavored butter
	salt
	pepper

Remove and discard the heavier outer leaves of the corn, leaving the paler, more tender leaves attached at the stem. Gently peel back husks and remove silk. Rub each ear of corn with 1 tbsp. (15 mL) softened butter. Pull attached husks back into place around ear of corn, pressing to close. Tear several discarded outer husks down into 1/2"-wide (1 cm) strips and tie them around each ear to close.

Submerge bound ears of corn in cold water to cover and soak 25 minutes. Drain and place on oiled grill. Grill corn 15–18 minutes, turning several times. Remove from grill and untie. Slather with additional butter, season with salt and pepper and enjoy!

GRILLED RADICCHIO

For a show-stopping first course, slip a thick piece of smoked Mozzarella cheese between the leaves of a halved head of radicchio, dip briefly in a pungent vinaigrette and grill in minutes. The contrasting flavors of the slightly charred, bitter, radicchio leaves and the warm, oozing melt of smoky cheese is simply delicious. Serve with country Italian bread, and a cruet of fruity olive oil to pass around. Serves 4.

2 full heads	fresh radicchio, cut in half vertically
4 slices	smoked Mozzarella cheese; each about 2 ounces (55 grams), 1/4" (1/2 cm) thick
1/2 cup (125 mL)	extra-virgin olive oil
1/4 cup (50 mL)	red wine vinegar
2 tbsp. (30 mL)	balsamic vinegar
2 large cloves	garlic, peeled and pressed
	salt
	freshly ground black pepper
	additional olive oil

Peel back the third leaf of each half-radicchio and tuck in the slice of cheese, concealing cheese within the layers. Press leaves back together.

Prepare coals to medium-hot, about 1 hour. Whisk together the olive oil, red wine vinegar, balsamic vinegar and garlic until emulsified in a small, shallow bowl. Set aside.

Lightly oil the grill and place 4" (10 cm) above coals. Quickly dip each stuffed radicchio into the oil mixture and place on grill. Grill radicchio about 2 minutes on each side, or just until lightly charred and cheese just begins to soften and melt. Remove from grill and serve immediately on warmed plates. Salt and pepper to taste, and pass a cruet of additional olive oil to drizzle over each serving.

SMOKY BAKED BLACK BEANS

*These black beans make a delicious Latin or Southwest addition to barbecue.
Serve with grilled steaks, ribs or chicken. Accompany with fresh salsa and a
dollop of sour cream, if desired.* **Serves 6.**

1 pound (500 grams)	dried black beans, rinsed in cold water
2 cups (500 mL)	rich beef stock
4 cups (1 litre)	cold water
3 whole dried	bay leaves
3 large cloves	garlic, peeled and slivered
1 large	onion, diced
1 tsp. (5 mL)	cumin seed
2 sticks	whole cinnamon, each 3" (7 cm) long
1/2 tsp. (2 mL)	ground cloves
1 tsp. (5 mL)	cracked black peppercorns
1	smoked ham hock, rind attached, cracked in 2 places
1 tsp. (5 mL)	salt (or to taste)
	minced fresh parsley
	diced red onion

Combine all ingredients, except for the salt, parsley and red onion, in a
deep 3-quart (1 1/2-litre) casserole, preferably crockery. Bury the
cracked ham hock in the center of the mixture. Place casserole, tightly
covered, in a preheated 275° F. (140° C.) oven. Bake until beans are
tender and water is absorbed. Stir occasionally. Total cooking time will
be approximately 6 hours or longer.

Serve beans warm. Sprinkle with minced parsley and diced red onion.

CONFETTI CORN MUFFINS

These zesty corn muffins make a terrific accompaniment to barbecued ribs, chicken and steaks. Simple to put together, they can bake while the main event is grilling. Pop from the pans to a basket, and serve very hot with lots of sweet butter. **Makes 1 dozen.**

1 cup (250 mL)	yellow cornmeal
3/4 cup (175 mL)	all-purpose flour
3 tbsp. (45 mL)	sugar
1/2 tsp. (2 mL)	salt
1 tbsp. (15 mL)	baking powder
1 cup (250 mL)	buttermilk
1 large	egg, beaten
4 tbsp. (60 mL)	melted butter
2 tbsp. (30 mL)	diced roasted peppers
2 tbsp. (30 mL)	diced pimiento

Grease 12 muffin cups. Preheat oven to 400° F. (200° C.). Sift together the cornmeal, flour, sugar, salt and baking powder. Whisk together the buttermilk, beaten egg and melted butter. Quickly combine both mixtures, mixing well. Finally, stir in the diced peppers and pimiento.

Spoon batter into prepared muffin cups. Bake on center rack in the preheated oven 20–25 minutes until golden brown and muffins spring back when pressed lightly on top. Remove from oven, allow to cool in pan 5 minutes. Turn out into cloth-lined basket, and serve at once with butter.

HERBED BUTTERMILK BISCUITS

These oversized, soft and airy, herb-flecked biscuits are great with barbecued ribs or chicken. Bake while meat is grilling, so that hot biscuits may be served right from the oven. Biscuits are one thing that can't wait! Serve with lots of sweet butter. **Makes 1 dozen.**

4 cups (1 litre)	all-purpose flour
1 tbsp. (15 mL) *plus*	
2 tsp. (10 mL)	baking powder
2 tsp. (10 mL)	baking soda
1 tsp. (5 mL)	salt
2 tsp. (10 mL)	sugar
6 tbsp. (90 mL) *each*	chilled butter and solid shortening
2 tbsp. (30 mL) *each*	minced fresh chives, dillweed, parsley
2 cups (500 mL)	buttermilk

Preheat oven to 425° F. (220° C.). Sift together the flour, baking powder, baking soda, salt and sugar in a deep mixing bowl. Cut in the chilled butter and solid shortening until mixture resembles coarse crumbs. Stir in the minced herbs. Make a well in the center and add the buttermilk. Stir quickly, just until mixture is moistened and forms a soft ball.

Generously flour hands and work surface. Turn dough out and knead gently 12 turns, so that dough is soft and "pillowy." Gently roll dough out to a 1" (2.5 cm) thickness. Cut with round cutter into 12 biscuits. Place on ungreased baking sheet, with sides of biscuits barely touching. Bake in center of preheated oven 15–18 minutes, or until light golden brown and doubled in height. Remove from oven, allow to sit on baking sheet 3 minutes and serve piping hot.

BARBECUED BAKED APPLES

*Baked apples are wonderful done on the open grill. Place them over ashen-white coals after meat has been grilled and cook during mealtime for instant dessert! Serve these splendid apples warm, with a thick pour of heavy, rich cream, or a scoop of rich vanilla ice cream. **Serves 6.***

6 large	baking apples (Rome Beauty, Granny Smith, Golden Delicious), cored
6 tbsp. (90 mL)	butter
6 tbsp. (90 mL)	brown sugar, packed
1 tsp. (5 mL)	ground cinnamon
1/2 tsp. (2 mL)	ground nutmeg
pinch	ground cloves
1/3 cup (75 mL)	finely chopped walnuts
2 tsp. (10 mL)	finely grated lemon rind
pinch	salt
6 tbsp. (90 mL)	Bourbon or Brandy (optional)
	heavy cream or vanilla ice cream

Cut squares of heavy-duty foil large enough to bring up around apple and twist closed. Cut squares of baking parchment to match. Line foil squares with parchment squares, and place 1 cored apple in center of each square. Fill cavity of each apple with 1/2 tbsp. (7 mL) butter.

Toss together the brown sugar, cinnamon, nutmeg, cloves, walnuts, lemon rind and pinch salt. Fill apple cavities evenly with mixture. Top each apple with remaining 1/2 tbsp. (7 mL) butter. Spoon 1 tbsp. (15 mL) Bourbon or Brandy over each apple, if desired.

Carefully bring up sides of parchment-lined foil, and twist closed at top to seal packet. Leave a bit of air-space around apple to allow for expansion.

Have coals prepared to ashen white, about 1 hour. Place apples on an oiled grill, around outer perimeter and cook about 40 minutes (if on a covered grill) and about 1 hour or longer (if on an open grill). Test one apple with a thin skewer; it should be very soft and tender.

Remove apples from grill, and allow to rest 20 minutes before opening. Open each apple carefully over shallow dessert dishes, being careful to catch all the wonderful, syrupy juices. Place each apple in center of dish. Serve just barely warm, with heavy cream, softly whipped cream or a scoop of vanilla ice cream.

BEST-EVER GARLIC BREAD

No barbecue feast would be complete without a great loaf of crisp, buttery garlic bread. Nothing will disappear quite as fast—so make several loaves, and prepare for seconds! **Serves 6.**

1 pound (500 grams)	loaf French or sourdough bread
1/2 pound (250 grams)	butter, softened to room temperature
3 cloves	garlic, peeled and pressed
3 tbsp. (45 mL)	mixed fresh herbs
or 1 tbsp. (15 mL)	mixed dried herbs
	(*select from oregano, thyme, marjoram, basil, rosemary, dill, chives, parsley)
2 tbsp. (30 mL)	Parmesan cheese, freshly grated

Slice bread in half horizontally. Combine the softened butter, garlic, mixed (or dried) herbs, and Parmesan cheese. Blend thoroughly. Spread flavored butter over cut sides of bread halves, spreading to all edges. Press halves back together lightly. Wrap in double aluminum foil. *Bread may be refrigerated overnight at this point. Bring bread to room temperature before baking.

Preheat oven 10 minutes at 350° F. (180° C.). Bake bread on center rack 20 minutes, until hot and crispy on the outside. Remove foil. Slice bread crosswise into generous pieces using a sharp serrated knife. Serve at once.

INDEX